25 YEARS ON ITV

ITV Books
&
Michael Joseph

Published by Independent Television Books Ltd
247 Tottenham Court Road, London W1P 0AU
and
Michael Joseph Ltd, 44 Bedford Square, London WC1B 3DU

© Independent Television Books Ltd, 1980

Cased edition: ISBN 0 900727 81 0
Paperback edition: ISBN 0 900727 80 2

Printed and bound by William Clowes (Beccles) Ltd,
Beccles and London

25 YEARS ON ITV

Compiled and produced by
ITV Books and TVTimes

ITV Books
&
Michael Joseph

FOREWORD

by SIR BRIAN YOUNG

Director General of the
Independent Broadcasting Authority

At the start, ITV was an ugly duckling. Lord Reith thought it was a grave mistake. Winston Churchill said it was "a tin penny Punch and Judy show." Even the advertisers, who were said to have conspired to give it birth, deserted it. Parliament passed the Independent Television Act in 1954; a year of planning and a year of transmission later, the whole system was close to financial ruin.

But the viewers seemed to like it. And in 1956 the two main transmitters in the North, Winter Hill and Emley Moor, were completed. Now Independent Television could reach more than half the population; now not only the viewers but the advertisers wanted it. Not for the first and not for the last time, it was the unknown engineers operating behind the scenes who made the breakthrough – though few people thanked them. Independent Television, almost over night, became financially successful – too successful, some said, for its own good reputation.

Making it regional helped. However hard it tried, the BBC remained a national organisation, London-based. But first Granada, then STV, Southern, Anglia and all the other regional companies soon made it plain that this was a different kind of television system, where not all the decisions were taken in the capital; and regional audiences soon identified with their companies. ITN showed that a news organisation could be lively, but also serious. *Coronation Street* showed how to be popular without losing quality. The companies were genuinely interested in politics, in religion, and in education. There were new advances in political broadcasting, like the coverage of the Rochdale by-election; there was *Armchair Theatre;* there were arts magazines like *Tempo.*

But few of ITV's merits appealed to the Government-appointed Pilkington Committee. They noticed the glitter more than the effective reaching out to people.

Nearly 1,300 ft of tubular steel, the Emley Moor mast which brought ITV to Yorkshire was the highest structure in Britain in 1956.

Arts programmes attract only minority audiences but even a minority audience is large on ITV; a Glyndebourne production of Mozart's opera, **The Marriage of Figaro** was watched by 3 million viewers. (Southern)

To them, ITV stood for American films and film series, and for a deplorable number of people enjoying *Sunday Night at the London Palladium* and wrestling on Saturday afternoon. They were right in a way; ITV had put first the winning of popular affection.

There followed a new Act of Parliament, and in 1968 the original contracts came to an end. It is the Authority's responsibility to appoint, and occasionally to disappoint, the programme companies. The largest county in Britain, Yorkshire, seemed to warrant the appointment of its own company to contribute to the network. The arrangements for London were altered, bringing to life another new company. Promising new talents emerged in Wales and the West. But, above all, the range of programmes continued to expand, with the Authority's encouragement. *News at Ten* gave television news the prestige of the most serious of newspapers. Current affairs programmes brought a

The Unknown Famine, a report by Jonathan Dimbleby for the current affairs series **This Week** about starvation in Ethiopia led to £5 million in aid being raised in Britain. (Thames)

News at Ten was the first regular half-hour news programme on a major channel; Alastair Burnet was its first newscaster and has remained ITV's man for big news occasions. (ITN)

new cutting-edge to television journalism. The standards of writing, of performance and of production to which we were accustomed in the single play were extended to series like *Edward the Seventh* – and colour helped. ITV's documentary programmes (some of them produced by regional companies) won much praise. Masterpieces in opera and drama became a regular part of the output. Sports coverage – long a weakness – was extended and improved.

ITV was of course wholly financed by advertising: yet many people came to see that it was not a purely "commercial" system of broadcasting. The Authority, a state corporation, stands at the head of the system. Programme companies make programmes, but only the Authority can broadcast them through its network of transmitters. It makes the final judgments about impartiality, and taste, and decency. It controls the schedules – the weekly and quarterly "timetables" of television. It exercises strict controls over the amount, distribution and content of the advertisements. There are real, and major, differences between a

Edward the Seventh brought a new distinction to drama series; Timothy West played the King and Helen Ryan his Queen. (ATV)

"commercial" broadcasting system and public service broadcasting financed by advertising.

By the time of its 21st birthday in 1976, ITV had won national acclaim – and international too, as it became a major prizewinner and as its programmes were seen regularly in many parts of the world, including the United States. Programmes like *Upstairs, Downstairs* and *The World at War* became world famous. And, with the help of extended hours, a change in the levy, and new involvement of the IBA in programme planning, the battle for full recognition and esteem was won. British television – BBC and ITV – was widely agreed to provide the "least worst" television service in the world.

The uncertainties of 1955, the Pilkington strictures of 1963, gave place to the Annan Committee's approval of 1977. In information, rather than in entertainment, it was ITV that led the BBC – a point that would have much surprised the original debaters. Only for trying new things, and for serving more audiences more fully, was something still needed – a further channel. And in 1980 the planning for that is beginning. The next 25 years should be better yet.

As uncompromisingly British as afternoon tea, **Upstairs, Downstairs** became one of ITV's biggest-selling programmes abroad. The saga ranged from the Edwardian era to the Twenties. (LWT)

Programme sales are a two-way trade and ITV introduced the best of American programmes to Britain, including Westerns such as **How The West Was Won.**

7

1955

ITV opened on September 22, after four years of argument. During this time, its advocates had decried BBC programmes as cosy and low budget, while its opponents had pointed to the American system and warned that commercial television would bring a lowering of standards in Britain.

But the Television Act of 1954 had set up the Independent Television Authority under Sir Kenneth–now Lord–Clark, Chairman of the Arts Council. And the ITA had devised a regional structure for ITV, and appointed programme companies.

Sir Winston Churchill, who had backed the alternative service, had handed over the Premiership to Sir Anthony Eden by the time it started, while Clement Attlee was about to be succeeded as Labour leader by Hugh Gaitskell.

ITV's impact was immediate. The public were fascinated by its newscasters, cash quiz shows, American programmes, and commercials.

But ITV was available only in the London area, and by the end of the year reached a mere 12.5 per cent of the homes in the country.

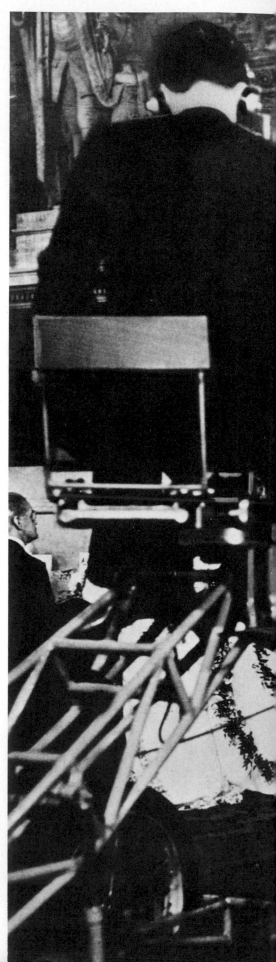

ITV was officially opened at 7.15 pm on September 22, when a dinner to mark the occasion was transmitted from the Guildhall, London. Speeches to welcome the new service were made by Sir Kenneth Clark; the Lord Mayor, Sir Seymour Howard; and the Postmaster General, Dr. Charles Hill, later Chairman successively of the ITA and BBC.

The Scarlet Pimpernel was among ITV's early programmes to prove popular. Marius Goring starred as Baroness Orczy's swashbuckling hero. (Associated-Rediffusion)

ITV launched big-name variety in its first week, with **Sunday Night at the London Palladium.** The show was compered by Tommy Trinder, starred Gracie Fields, and featured The Tiller Girls. (ATV)

The Adventures of Robin Hood, with Richard Greene in the title role, was to become one of television's most successful film series. (ATV)

The first commercial was transmitted at 8.12 on opening night when an urgent voice proclaimed: "It's tingling fresh, it's fresh as ice…it's Gibbs SR toothpaste."

Former bandleader Jack Jackson introduced **Variety,** a programme for opening night which presented "some of the stars who will be featured regularly on ITV…" Among them were Reg Dixon and Harry Secombe. (ATV)

11

1955

Boris Karloff played **Col. March of Scotland Yard** in a crime series about the Yard's "Department of Queer Complaints". (ATV)

Chris Chataway (24), the record-breaking athlete, read ITN's first news at 10pm on September 22. He was the newscaster for their main programmes. (ITN)

Margaret Leighton,
Sir John Gielgud and
Dame Edith Evans
appeared in a scene
from **The Importance
of Being Earnest,**
one of three excerpts
from plays on ITV's
gala inaugural night.
(Associated-
Rediffusion)

Godfrey Winn invited viewers to write to him about their domestic problems; these were scripted and presented with his solutions in **As Others See Us.** (Associated-Rediffusion)

Fanny's Kitchen was the title of ITV's first cookery series. Although it was presented by Fanny Cradock–assisted in later series by husband Johnny– she was introduced as Phyllis Cradock. (Associated-Rediffusion)

Michaela and Armand Denis were the stars of ITV's first wildlife series, which they filmed in Africa. (ATV)

Double Your Money, Hughie Green's cash quiz, was to become one of the most popular programmes on ITV. (Associated-Rediffusion)

Michael Miles introduced his first **Take Your Pick** quiz show—complete with "yes-no" interlude—on ITV's second night. (Associated-Rediffusion)

15

Mick and Montmorency starred in a series of 15-minute comedy programmes; behind the pseudonyms were Charlie Drake and Jack Edwardes. (Associated-Rediffusion)

Actor-turned-prod
Douglas Fairba
introduced the fi
his series of
dramas, **Dou
Fairbanks Prese**
(Associa
Rediffus

ITV introduced **Free Speech**, political cross-talk between Sir Robert (now Lord) Boothby, W. J. Brown, Michael Foot and A. J. P. Taylor. The new programme was similar to the BBC's **In the News,** in which the four appeared. This had been dropped when the main political parties attempted to substitute orthodox representatives. Boxing promoter Jack Solomons introduced action from big fights in **Jack Solomons' Scrapbook.**

ITV's first daily serial was **Sixpenny Corner,** a 15-minute drama shown weekday mornings. It starred Patricia Dainton and Howard Pays as garage owners.

Popular American programmes on ITV included the crime series **Dragnet,** the comedy **I Love Lucy,** and the Westerns **Gun Law** and **Hopalong Cassidy.**

1956

ITV spread to the Midlands and North, and by the end of the year was in more than a quarter of the homes in the country. Its programmes topped the ratings, but advertisers were still wary of spending £1,000 a minute on the new medium while its coverage was still somewhat limited.

Understandably, many ITV programmes were dedicated to mass entertainment; only 19 per cent of the output was classed by the ITA as "serious".

ATV took the initiative in obtaining permission from the Postmaster General to show religious programmes between 6 and 7.30 on Sunday evenings, when television had been shut down in order not to deter churchgoing. The first programme was **About Religion,** a series of interviews.

The Postmaster General also revoked the notorious Fourteen Day Rule, which had barred TV from discussing controversial subjects due for Parliamentary debate during the following fortnight.

Nasser seized the Suez Canal and Prime Minister Eden ordered an invasion of Egypt. Russia sent tanks to Hungary to crush demands for democracy.

Boyd QC, ITV's first courtroom drama series, was created by Jack Roffey and illustrated many facets of trials justice. It was so accurate that Michael Denison, who played the "silk", received invitations to address Law Society dinners... (Associated-Rediffusion)

1956

Among the many quiz shows of the period, **The 64,000 Question** was derived from an American series. The British show featured Jerry Desmonde as quizmaster and ex-Det. Supt. Robert Fabian was "custodian of the questions". (ATV)

The Adventures of Sir Lancelot concerned the legendary knights of King Arthur's round table. William Russell played the romantic hero. (ATV)

Brian Inglis was a frequent presenter of **What the Papers Say,** TV's weekly survey of how Fleet Street has treated the news. (Granada)

McDonald Hobley introduced **Yakity-Yak,** a panel game that would attract little support from the Women's Lib group. It was subtitled "the dizzy show" and encouraged the six girl panellists to give silly answers to the questions. (ATV)

1956

The Count of Monte Cristo, a series based on the Dumas story, starred George Dolenz as the Count. (ATV)

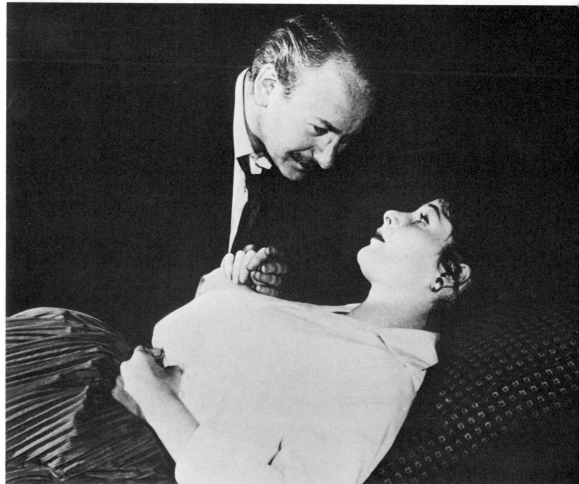

Plays of this period were usually adapted from stage successes, as there was no corps of established playwrights. **The Outsider,** first of the **Armchair Theatre** productions, was adapted from the 1923 Dorothy Brandon drama about medical ethics, and starred Adrienne Corri and David Kossoff. (ABC)

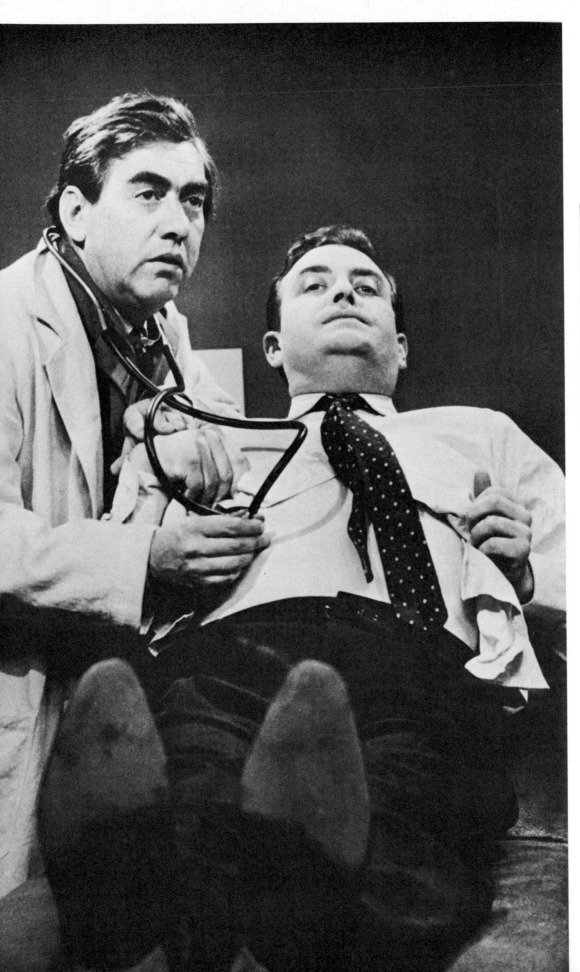

Ludovic Kennedy's long association with ITV began when he was invited to replace Chris Chataway as one of ITN's regular newscasters. (ITN)

After his spectacular success on BBC Radio, comic Tony Hancock transferred his talents to television. **The Tony Hancock Show** was the first of many series he made for ITV. (Associated-Rediffusion)

23

1956

Sport was still comparatively sparse on television, but in **Jack Solomons' Scrapbook**, the fight promoter showed film of famous bouts. In 1956 – the year when Rocky Marciano retired as undefeated World Heavyweight Champion – Solomons recalled Marciano's defeat of Archie Moore the previous year. (ATV)

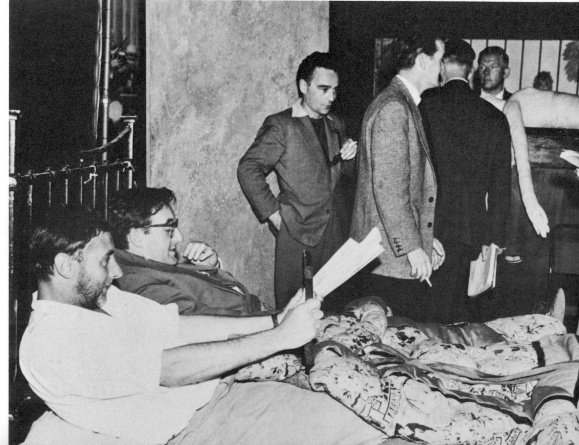

The Goons brought a new and anarchic humour to radio; with **Son of Fred**, Spike Milligan and Peter Sellers made an early attempt to do the same on television. (Associated-Rediffusion)

Catherine Boyle appeared in a panel game, **I've Got a Secret!** Here she was inaugurating a studio switchboard with a call to Ben Lyon, Chairman of the programme. (Associated-Rediffusion)

Robert Shaw played a swashbuckling, ex-pirate captain in **The Buccaneers,** and was hailed as "one of the most exciting romantic discoveries of the year." (ATV)

Stealing scenes from Arthur Askey isn't easy, but Sabrina did so in **Before Your Very Eyes**; her vital statistics caused nationwide comment. (Associated-Rediffusion)

Domestic comedies featuring real-life husband and wife teams were popular on TV at this time. Among them was **My Husband and I**, starring Evelyn Laye and Frank Lawton. (Associated-Rediffusion)

In **The Arthur Haynes Show**, written by Johnny Speight, the comedian appeared regularly as a tramp who discomfited authority. (ATV)

The future star of **Crossroads** introduced her own series, **Tea With Noele Gordon,** in which she talked to guests about life in the theatre.
The Guild of Television Producers and Directors voted ITN newscaster Chris Chataway the TV Personality of the year. **This Week** began, packing as many as six contrasting items into 30 minutes. Hughie Green introduced **Opportunity Knocks!** which had been a radio favourite for many years. Among the new shows from America were **The Errol Flynn Theatre,** and **Highway Patrol,** starring Broderick Crawford. This series gave rise to the catchphrase "Ten-four," Crawford's acknowledgement of radio messages. Comedy stars with their own series included Alfred Marks, Joan and Leslie Randall, Dora Bryan, rubber-faced Libby Morris, and Bernard Braden and Barbara Kelly. **My Wildest Dream** featured Marks, David Nixon, Tommy Trinder and Terry-Thomas.

1957

In the year Harold Macmillan replaced Anthony Eden as Premier—and went on to launch the era of "You've never had it so good"—the finances of ITV began to improve. As ITV spread into central Scotland, the revenue of the pioneer companies increased, though their losses were to total £11 million in the first 18 months.

Although determined never to lose contact with the mass audience, ITV became the first channel to screen programmes for schools. It also introduced outside broadcasts of Sunday morning church services, beginning with a Battle of Britain drumhead service from RAF, Biggin Hill.

The "toddlers' truce"—a shutdown of both ITV and BBC Television between 6 pm and 7 pm so mothers could put small children to bed—came to an end.

And on Saturday nights, television continued until midnight. The extra hour was used to show a feature film.

A combined TV and radio licence went up by £1 to £4.

Emergency-Ward 10, a twice-weekly serial about hospital life, began a successful 10-year run, and won a production award from the Guild of Television Producers and Directors. (ATV)

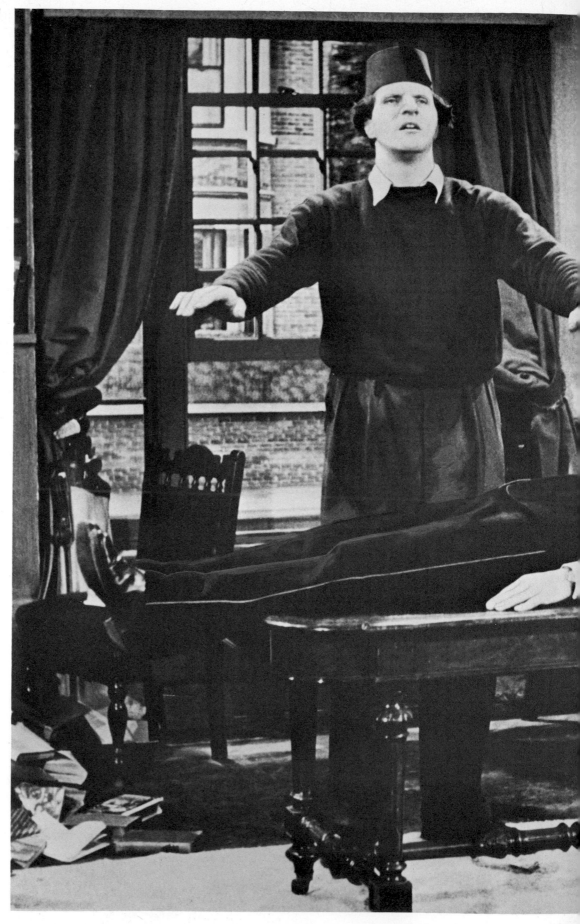

Cooper–Life With Tommy, introduced the comic conjurer in his own series. It was the beginning of an association with ITV that has continued. (Associated-Rediffusion)

The interview which Robin Day conducted with President Nasser in Cairo was one of the most significant to date. It took place soon after the Suez crisis, while Britain was still technically at war with Egypt. Day was Guild of Television Producers and Directors' TV Personality of the Year. (ITN)

Making his debut in **Murder Bag,** Det. Insp. Tom Lockhart, played by Raymond Francis, went on to appear in **No Hiding Place.** In the 10-year period, he rose to the rank of Chief Superintendent. (Associated-Rediffusion)

1957

Lunch Box, a music show with Noele Gordon as hostess, introduced in the Midlands at the end of 1956, achieved recognition when it was shown on the network. (ATV)

The first quiz show with a noughts and crosses formula was **Criss Cross Quiz**, introduced by Jeremy Hawk. (Granada)

Actor John Slater introduced one of the first advertising magazines, **Slater's Bazaar,** in which commercials were interwoven with light entertainment. (ATV)

Mark Saber was one of the first British series to be sold to America. It starred Donald Gray as a one-armed detective. (ATV)

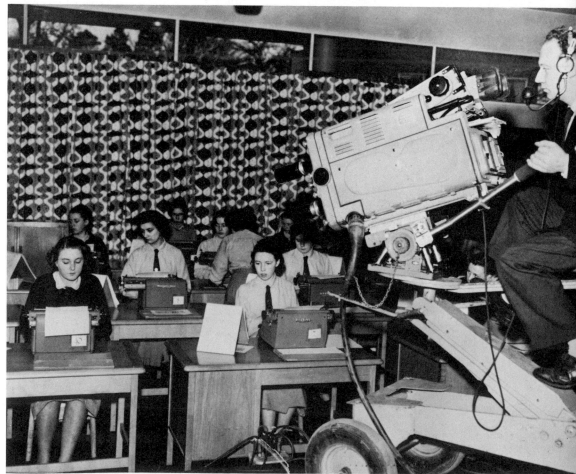

To celebrate a visit to Paris by the Queen, London and the French capital were linked by **Telerama.** Showbusiness stars were introduced by Leslie Mitchell in London and Art Buchwald in Paris. (Associated-Rediffusion)

PROPRIÉTÉ PRIVÉE
de l'ENTENTE FLUVIALE

DÉFENSE

Eighty schools viewed **Looking and Seeing,** the first programme for schools. The new service resulted from the initiative of Paul Adorian, the Managing Director of Associated-Rediffusion.

Theatre techniques, with close-ups of actors in the studio, were used in the production of **Shadow Squad,** a series starring Rex Garner as a Flying Squad officer turned private crimebuster. (Associated-Rediffusion)

Former Goons Peter Sellers and Michael Bentine joined forces for the zany comedy series, **Yes, It's the Cathode-Ray Tube Show.** (Associated-Rediffusion)

Jim's Inn, the most popular advertising magazine, featured Jimmy Hanley as the landlord of a village pub. These magazines were to be banned by Parliament in 1963. (Associated-Rediffusion)

Another quiz show of the year was **Bury Your Hatchet,** in which couples with a grudge against each other competed for money prizes. The hosts were Bob Monkhouse and Denis Goodwin. (ATV)

The Army Game was destined to become one of ITV's biggest situation comedy successes. William Hartnell played the CSM. (Granada)

Sir Ivone Kirkpatrick, former Permanent Under Secretary of State at the Foreign Office, succeeded Sir Kenneth Clark as Chairman of the ITA. For the first time, the Queen made her traditional Christmas Day broadcast on television.

John Grierson, acknowledged father of the documentary film, wrote and introduced **This Wonderful World,** which examined documentary films from all over the world. The series—it continued until 1966—was the new Scottish Television's first regular contribution to the network.

Huw Thomas, who had joined ITN's newscasting team at the end of 1956, established himself as a popular ITV personality.

The first successful videotape recorders were imported from America. Television, until now live or on film, would soon be able to record programmes for showing at a later date. Studios could be employed around the clock, and artists appear whenever they were available.

1958

Television finally superseded radio as the more popular home entertainment. This development was helped by ITV's expansion into South Wales, the West and Southern England. There were now 6.5 million homes with ITV reception.

As ITV gained confidence in holding the mass audience, it extended its range to include new arts programmes and original drama productions.

Political discussion on television had always ceased when an election campaign began, for fear of accusations that voters were being influenced. But while the BBC followed the accepted practice for the Rochdale by-election, Granada–after taking eminent legal advice–gave the campaign major coverage, and opened the way for today's comprehensive election coverage.

Nikita Khruschev took over in the Kremlin and Pope John in the Vatican. Pictures of the Pope's installation were transmitted live via Eurovision. Iceland extended her territorial fishing limits to 12 miles.

Fred Robinson created **The Larkins** for Scout concerts, but the Cockney family soon became national favourites when they were introduced to television. Peggy Mount and David Kossoff played Ada and Alf Larkin in the series. (ATV)

1958

The Sunday Break,
the brainchild of
Howard Thomas,
then Managing
Director of ABC,
was the first "pop"
religious show.
Set in a youth club,
with pop music
in the background, it
posed questions
of interest to young
people. (ABC)

Diana Dors and Alan
Melville were among
artists living or
working in the South
who were featured
in **Southern Rhapsody,**
a gala programme on
the opening night of
Southern Television.

Jackie Rae posed the questions, Marion Ryan was the resident singer, in **Spot the Tune.** (Granada)

People in Trouble, from kleptomaniacs to alcoholics, were interviewed by Dan Farson, labelled ITV's "Mr. Documentary". (Associated-Rediffusion)

Bruce Forsyth joined **Sunday Night at the London Palladium** as compere – direct from pierhead shows. He was the first artist to achieve stardom via this job. (ATV)

41

ITV presented its first coverage of an election campaign at the Rochdale by-election. Voters were interviewed in the streets and the candidates allotted equal studio time. (Granada)

The Outside Broadcast cameras introduced an unfamiliar sport when they showed Prince Philip playing in a polo match in Windsor Great Park. (Associated-Rediffusion)

Television returned to the Classics with the adventure series **Ivanhoe,** starring Roger Moore, described at the time as "practically unknown". (ATV)

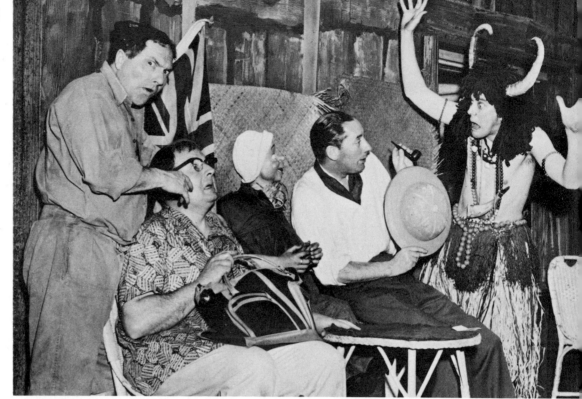

The ventriloquist Peter Brough introduced a new, walking Archie Andrews dummy when **Educating Archie** was moved from radio to television. Dick Emery was one of the regular cast. (Associated-Rediffusion)

The Verdict is Yours, a series of mock trials, had plots but no scripts. Actors playing witnesses and counsel improvised their lines. (Granada)

Granada Television maintained a film unit at London Zoo for their natural history programmes. Among them was **Zoo Time,** presented by Desmond Morris, then the Curator of Mammals. (Granada)

One of the most popular comedians in the country was Dave King, a regular celebrity in **Val Parnell's Saturday Spectacular.** (ATV)

Robert Beatty starred as a tough Canadian Mountie attached to Scotland Yard in **Dial 999,** a crime series aimed at the valuable American market. (ATV)

The State opening of Parliament by the Queen was televised for the first time. Robin Day was the commentator for ITV.

The Queen, accompanied by Prince Philip, paid her first visit to ITA's headquarters, then at Princes Gate, Kensington. Jack Good produced **Oh Boy!** ITV's first pop show for teenagers. There were major developments in ITV's coverage of the arts. **The Book Man** was the first television series devoted entirely to writers and their works. Sir Kenneth Clark presented a series entitled **Is Art Necessary?** Laurence Olivier made his television debut in Henrik Ibsen's **John Gabriel Borkman.** Many programmes were still transmitted live at this time. Among them were the **Armchair Theatre** plays. During the broadcast of **Underground,** one of the cast collapsed and died. While out of camera shot, the other actors were told that he had been taken ill and they would have to improvise; they carried on.

1959

The first General Election to be covered fully by television – due to ITV's innovatory coverage of the 1958 Rochdale by-election – returned Harold Macmillan to Downing Street for another term.

ITV expanded into North East England, East Anglia and Northern Ireland to reach a total of 8.6 million homes, more than 55 per cent of all those in the British Isles. By this time, ITV was watched by 70 per cent of those with a choice of viewing, and by June the ITA had repaid the £555,000 borrowed from the Postmaster General to start operations.

Fidel Castro seized power in Cuba, and civil war broke out in the Belgian Congo. Russia and America began training astronauts. At home, the first stretch of the M1 Motorway was opened.

Holiday Town Parade, a combined bathing beauty, fashion queen and male Adonis contest, with heats in seaside resorts, was shown on the national network after three years in the Midlands and North. (ABC)

Ed Murrow, the noted American journalist, spoke on the merits and defects of television in the first televised **Granada Lecture** at London's Guildhall. (Granada)

To mark the centenary of Isambard Kingdom Brunel's death, Peter Wyngarde portrayed him in the dramatised documentary, **Engineer Extraordinary.** (TWW)

Probation Officer was applauded for its authenticity: an episode on the after-care of prisoners was shown to members of both Houses of Parliament during the passage of the controversial Criminal Justice Bill. (ATV)

John Turner starred in **Knight Errant,** a drama series about a modern crusader who championed the oppressed. (Granada)

International stars Vittorio de Sica, Jack Hawkins, Dan Dailey and Richard Conte played **The Four Just Men** in a series based on the Edgar Wallace thriller. (ATV)

Domestic sketches, song and dance were the ingredients of **The Dickie Henderson Half Hour,** with Anthea Askey playing his wife. (Associated-Rediffusion)

Many celebrated actors and actresses were now making their TV debuts; here, Vivien Leigh was Sabina in Thornton Wilder's **The Skin of Our Teeth.** (Granada)

As the airlines began regular jet services, ITV launched **Skyport**, a drama series about the activities at an international airport. (Granada)

Alun Owen won the Guild of TV Producers and Directors' award for Best Scriptwriter, helped by his first TV play, **No Tram to Lime Street**, an **Armchair Theatre** play starring Jack Hedley and Billie Whitelaw. She was the Guild's TV Actress of the Year. (ABC)

Land of Song meant, of course, Wales and featured Welsh choirs and singers. Ivor Emmanuel was the star of this long running series. (TWW)

Bernard Braden and Huw Thomas introduced **Let's Go**, the first Saturday afternoon programme to visit sporting events around the country. Sir John Gielgud appeared in **A Day By the Sea** and Flora Robson in **Mother Courage**.

Mary Holland made her debut as Katie, the pretty housewife preparing lunch for her good-natured husband, Philip, in the Oxo commercials.

New American Westerns included **Have Gun – Will Travel**, starring Richard Boone.

1960

A committee under the chairmanship of Sir Harry Pilkington, the glass manufacturer, was set up to consider the future of broadcasting. Meanwhile, ITV extended into South East England and sales of its programmes abroad began to grow.

In the first year of the so-called Swinging Sixties, viewers saw TV confrontations swing it for John F. Kennedy in the United States presidential election. Princess Margaret married photographer Antony Armstrong-Jones. The courts freed Lady Chatterley's Lover for publication, and the News of the World serialised the memoirs of actress Diana Dors.

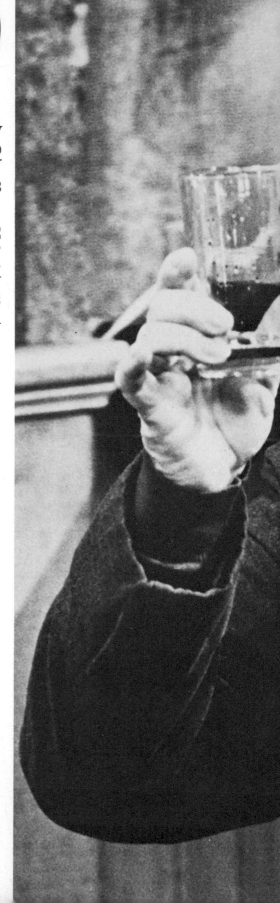

Coronation Street began – and the hair-netted, vinegary Ena Sharples, played by Violet Carson, was soon established as one of ITV's greatest characters ever. (Granada)

1960

Jean Clarke wiggled to stardom as one of the hostesses on **Double Your Money.** She said of her eye-catching walk: "I just can't help it." (Associated-Rediffusion)

Ingenious hoaxes such as this baffled victims of **Candid Camera.** Their various reactions were recorded by hidden cameras. (ABC)

The largest number of ITV cameras ever assembled for one event covered the wedding of Princess Margaret and Antony Armstrong-Jones.

Danger Man, one of ITV's most successful adventure series, starred Patrick McGoohan as a tough, globetrotting security agent. (ATV)

Arthur Christiansen, ex-Editor of the Daily Express, was editorial adviser to **Deadline Midnight,** a drama series set in Fleet Street. (ATV)

Ian Hendry played Dr. Geoffrey Brent in the drama series **Police Surgeon.** One year later, Hendry starred as the same character in the first of **The Avengers** series. (ABC)

The Canadian couple Barbara Kelly and Bernard Braden were in demand for many types of show. Here, they were appearing as themselves in the new comedy series **Rolling Stones.** (ATV)

Our House, a comedy series by Carry On film writer Norman Hudis, featured a boarding house and its bizarre group of residents. (ABC)

Moira Lister was the star of Flotsam and Jetsam, the first in the series Somerset Maugham Hour. (Associated-Rediffusion)

The Royal Variety Performance was televised for the first time. The Queen and Prince Philip were amused particularly by the Crazy Gang, who were to become regular favourites in the show. (ATV)

1960

The Derby was shown throughout Britain for the first time. ITV viewers watched Lester Piggott romp home on St. Paddy. (Associated-Rediffusion)

The Strange World of Gurney Slade was a whimsical rarity in television comedy. Surrounded by lovely girls, Anthony Newley spoke to trees and animals – and they answered. (ATV)

An early example of a "spin-off," **Bootsie and Snudge** followed **The Army Game**'s Bill Fraser and Alfie Bass into civilian life. (Granada)

Margot Fonteyn and Michael Somes danced in the Royal Ballet's production of Frederick Ashton's **Cinderella**. The television studio gave double the space of the stage at Covent Garden. (Granada)

The comedy series **Mess Mates** was set on a small cargo ship plying around Britain's coast. (Associated-Rediffusion)

The props department acquired genuine Victorian draper's trimmings for the eight-part series **Kipps,** adapted from H.G. Wells' novel by Clive Exton, and starring Brian Murray. (Granada)

Our Street, a seven-part documentary, examined life in a typical working class road in Camberwell, South East London. (Associated-Rediffusion)

Sunday Night at the London Palladium had become a national institution. Vicars even altered the times of evening services so the congregations could watch the show. Average audiences numbered 17 million, but Cliff Richard won 19.5 million, Max Bygraves 21 million, and Harry Secombe 22 million.

Diana Dors made her ITV drama debut in an **Armchair Theatre** play called **The Innocent.**

American imports included **77 Sunset Strip,** and the Western **Bonanza**.

Biggles, W. E. Johns' story for children about a flying ace, was adapted for television.

Twenty Questions, the animal, vegetable and mineral quiz, moved to ITV under the chairmanship of Stewart MacPherson.

1961

The television industry was concerned with technical questions regarding its future. An international conference allocated new UHF frequencies, making it possible for Britain to have new channels in addition to the existing ones on VHF. Other conferences sought in vain to agree on a common system of colour.

But the Government decided that colour should not be introduced until a third channel was in existence – on UHF – and the Continental 625 line standard had begun to replace the 405 line system.

Meanwhile, ITV expanded into South West England, North East Scotland and the Borders. The number of ITV homes rose to 11.3 million.

Current affairs and documentary programmes reflected a fast changing world – the first spaceman, Russia's Yuri Gagarin; the building of the Berlin Wall; South Africa becoming a republic, and Britain's application to join the Common Market.

The first programme in the award-winning natural history series, **Survival,** dealt with London's wildlife, including Hampstead Heath's fox families. (Anglia)

The **Avengers** began, with Ian Hendry as a doctor and Patrick Macnee an umbrella-wielding secret agent; the lovely, lethal judo girls were yet to make a debut. (ABC)

Set in a fictional London department store, **Harpers West One** was a drama series featuring Jan Holden. (ATV)

Family Solicitor attracted praise from the Law Society, who said: "For years we have waited for television to present a series like this." (Granada)

Without referring to maps or notes, A.J.P. Taylor delivered a highly praised series of lectures on the **First World War.** (ATV)

Sammy Davis Jr., now at the height of his popularity, came to Britain to star in **Sunday Night at the London Palladium**, and **Sammy Davis Meets the Girls**. (ATV)

The Earl of Harewood, Edinburgh Festival's Artistic Director, introduced the weekly arts series, **Tempo**, which was edited by Kenneth Tynan. (ABC)

1961

The trial of Soviet spies Peter and Helen Kroger, who were sentenced to 20 years imprisonment in the Portland secrets case, was followed by a documentary, **35 Cranley Drive.** (Granada)

The Quiet War, an incisive look at the guerilla struggle in Vietnam, was a British contribution to a series of films made for world-wide showing by Intertel. (Associated-Rediffusion)

Although renowned for realistic, modern drama, **Armchair Theatre** screened an award-winning fantasy on the theme of beauty and the beast, Alun Owen's **The Rose Affair**. (ABC)

1961

As America backed a military invasion to overthrow Cuba's Fidel Castro, ITV screened four documentaries about the country, entitled **Cuba...Si!** (Granada)

The trial of former Gestapo chief Adolf Eichmann, accused of crimes against humanity, took place in Jerusalem and was shown exclusively in Britain on ITV. (ATV)

The Duke of Kent's marriage to Katharine Worsley brought scenes of splendour to York Minster. Nine ITV commentators described the event.

The first in a series of exchange television programmes with Russia was the live transmission of the British Trade Fair opening in Moscow's Sokolniki Park.
An early documentary in the series **Into Europe** asked: "Will farmers survive if Britain joins the Common Market?"
The Inauguration of John F. Kennedy as President of the United States was shown in a one-hour programme the following day.
William Franklyn – not yet associated with the Schw... commercials – starred as a British agent in South America in **Top Secret**.

1962

There were significant developments in television news. Telstar, the first satellite capable of relaying television across the Atlantic, was launched and British viewers saw the first live pictures from America.

And when President Kennedy confronted Khrushchev in the week-long Cuban missiles crisis, it was to television that Britons turned to discover whether it was to be peace or war. By the end of the year, television was the main source of news for 52 per cent of the population – double the figure in 1957.

The Pilkington Committee's report approved the BBC's television service but was critical of some aspects of ITV. The Government rejected the Committee's recommendation that the ITA should take over the planning of schedules and selling of advertising, but it awarded the third channel to the BBC.

Meanwhile, ITV moved into North and West Wales, the Channel Isles and Ulster to become available to 96 per cent of the population.

Thalidomide was withdrawn after causing deformities in babies, Britain and France agreed to build a supersonic airliner, Concorde.

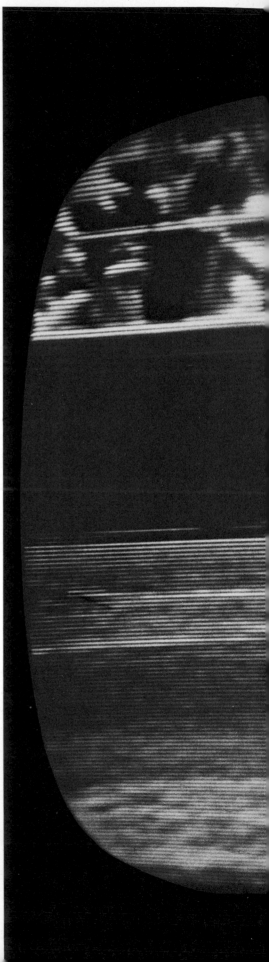

First transmissions via the new American satellite, Telstar, showed baseball from Chicago, an excerpt from a production of **Macbeth** in Ontario, and a Presidential press conference in Washington. (ITN)

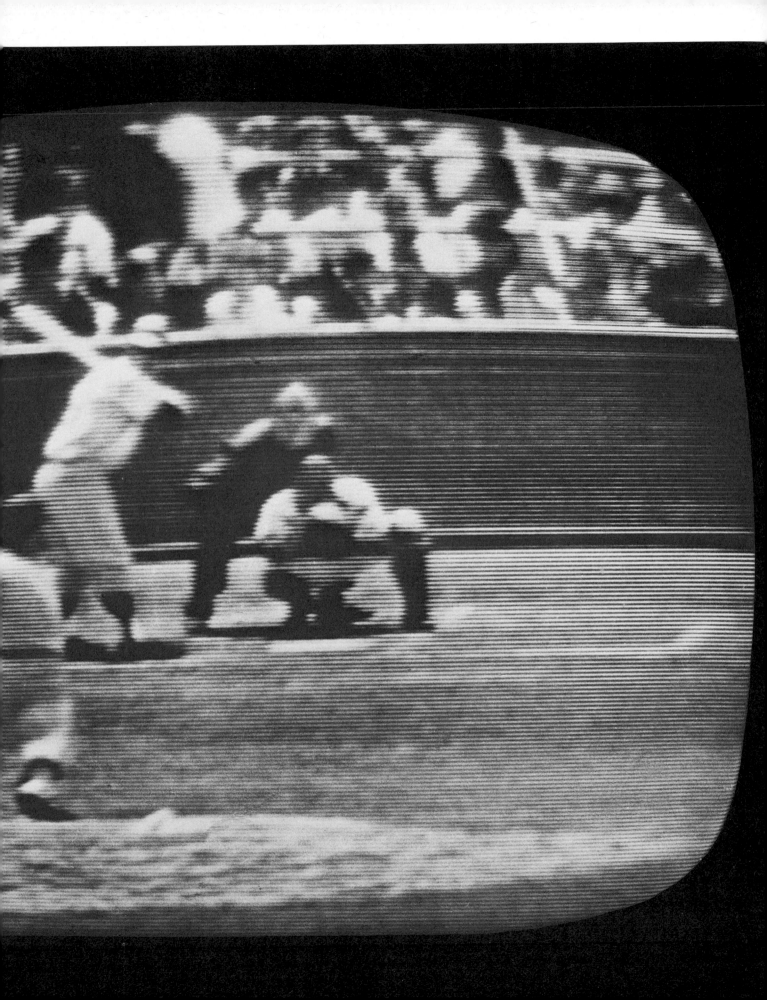

The Piraikon Greek
Tragedy Theatre
Company performed
Electra, the 2,500-year-
old play by Sophocles...
in their native tongue.
(Associated-
Rediffusion)

The hero of **Man of the World** was a photo journalist, played by Craig Stevens, which gave an opportunity to dress the female characters in chic clothes designed by the Fashion House Group. (ATV)

Norman Vaughan was Bruce Forsyth's successor as compere of **Sunday Night at the London Palladium** and delighted audiences with funny mannerisms and the catchphrases "dodgy" and "swinging". (ATV)

For years, Eric Morecambe and Ernie Wise have ended their shows with a running gag. In **The Morecambe and Wise Show** – written by Dick Hills and Sid Green – they always attempted to leave the stage by a door that was too small. (ATV)

1962

University Challenge was one of the most demanding quiz shows to date. Offering no individual prizes, it featured teams of students answering questions posed by the erudite Bamber Gascoigne. (Granada)

The Saint, based on the character created by Leslie Charteris, came to ITV as a series of hour-long thrillers, with Roger Moore starring in the title role. It ran for seven years and was sold to 80 countries. (ATV)

Armchair Theatre commissioned Robert Muller's first play, **Afternoon of a Nymph,** with Janet Munro playing a film starlet and Ian Hendry as a director. (ABC)

A new comedy series written by Jack Rosenthal and Harry Driver, **Bulldog Breed** starred Donald Churchill as Tom Bowler, an engaging young man with a gift for creating chaos. (Granada)

Short stories by **Saki**
(H. H. Munro) were
adapted as a series
for television and
played by a company
which included
husky-voiced Fenella
Fielding. (Granada)

The Guild of Television Producers and Directors conferred a special award for news programmes on Geoffrey Cox, Editor of ITN. Ballet idol Rudolf Nureyev topped the bill of **Sunday Night at the London Palladium.** Prince Philip appeared in **This Week** to report on his tour of South America. A TWW programme on **Dylan Thomas** won a Hollywood Motion Picture Academy award as the best short subject documentary. **Thank Your Lucky Stars** won an award from Melody Maker magazine as the best TV pop show. A new quiz show with a crossword puzzle formula was **Take a Letter,** with Robert Holness as Chairman.

Honor Blackman ined **The Avengers** as attractive judo rl Mrs. Cathy Gale – d caused a fashion sensation with er leather suits and high boots. (ABC)

1963

The nation was gripped by Beatlemania but, following the Pilkington Committee's strictures, ITV increased the proportion of programmes classed as "serious" by the ITA to 37 per cent.

The wider range included the first adult education on British TV, with Sunday morning lessons in English and French, and a new current affairs series, **World in Action**, was introduced.

Lord Hill of Luton, the wartime radio doctor, succeeded Sir Ivone Kirkpatrick as Chairman of the ITA. Harold Macmillan yielded the Premiership to Sir Alec Douglas-Home. Harold Wilson became leader of the Labour party on the death of Hugh Gaitskell. War Minister John Profumo resigned, Pope John died, and President Kennedy was assassinated.

His funeral was shown live in Britain via Early Bird, successor to Telstar and the first satellite to remain stationary and be available for use at all times.

Beginning as a drama series concerning shopfloor workers in an aircraft factory, **The Plane Makers** was soon preoccupied with boardroom politics. Patrick Wymark played the ruthless Managing Director, John Wilder, who was the prototype for a variety of modern anti-heroes. (ATV)

1963

Central character in
The Human Jungle
was a psychiatrist,
played by Herbert
Lom, whose readiness
to become involved
in his patients'
problems provided
the basis for a
unique series. (ABC)

Spies, secret agents, saboteurs and undercover men were the heroes of **Espionage,** a series of 26 self-contained dramas. (ATV)

The first series of **Our Man at St. Mark's** starred Leslie Phillips as the vicar. Donald Sinden later took the role. (Associated-Rediffusion)

Men of Our Time was a documentary series that examined world leaders of the 20th century. Included was an assessment by James Cameron of Mahatma Gandhi, the passive revolutionary who founded present-day India. (Granada)

The Victorians, eight plays originally presented on stage in the 19th century, was performed by the Company of Seven, a TV repertory group assembled for the series. (Granada)

1963

Few plays have won the honours accorded to **The Lover,** a stylish sex comedy by Harold Pinter. It brought him The Guild of Television Producers and Directors' Best Script award, while Vivien Merchant and Alan Badel were the Guild's Best Actress and Actor, and director Joan Kemp–Welch won the Desmond Davis award for outstanding creative work. The play also won the coveted Prix Italia. (Associated-Rediffusion)

The urge to get away was exploited by **Crane,** an adventure series about a Briton, played by Patrick Allen, who gave up his job to run a cafe, a boat and a smuggling business in Morocco. (Associated-Rediffusion)

Love Story was an example of the trend away from single plays to anthologies. The series' common theme was romance, involving all classes and ages. Roger Livesey appeared in the leading role in **Raymond's Italian Woman**; Lea Padovani was the object of his affections. (ATV)

1963

ITV's biggest outside broadcast since the marriage of Princess Margaret was another royal wedding, that of Princess Alexandra to the Hon. Angus Ogilvy. Brian Connell was the commentator in Westminster Abbey and a total of 29 TV cameras was used.

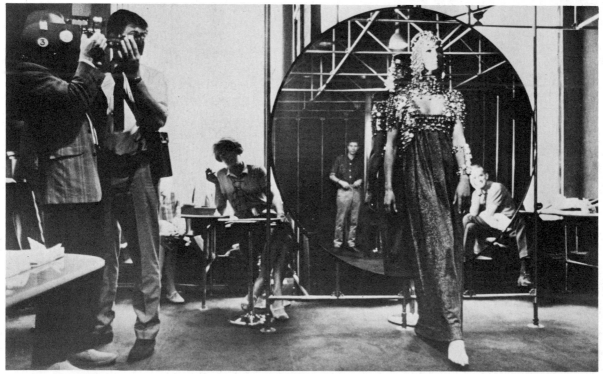

The compelling style of **World in Action** was due largely to producer Tim Hewat. An early programme, **High Fashion,** looked at the haute couture industry. (Granada)

The world mourned the death of John F. Kennedy, whose promising presidency was ended by an assassin's bullet. The funeral was given special ITV coverage.

On the Braden Beat, a unique mixture of entertainment and investigations into consumer complaints, won Bernard Braden a Guild of Television Producers and Directors' award for performance in factual programmes. Geoffrey Cox, Editor of ITN, was honoured for the second year in succession, receiving the Television Society's silver medal for production.

A two-and-three-quarter hour production of **War and Peace,** with a cast of 40, won Granada an Emmy award. Advertising magazines were banned by Parliament; commercials were subsequently confined to natural breaks.

A year after he had announced his retirement from show-business, Charlie Drake changed his mind and began a new comedy series, **The Charlie Drake Show.** In response to viewer demand, Leonard White, the new producer of **Armchair Theatre,** moved away from "kitchen sink" drama to a policy of star names and popular plays.

97

1964

The Television Act extended the life of Independent Television – originally licensed for 10 years – to 1976, and gave the ITA increased powers over programmes and advertising.

Before deciding the programme contractors for the new period, the Authority interviewed 22 groups of applicants, including the existing contractors. It then reappointed the existing companies until 1967, by which time it hoped ITV would be operating the proposed fourth channel.

While the BBC began transmissions on its second, 625 line channel, a levy was imposed on ITV's advertising revenue. This achieved its object, cutting the profits of the programme companies and taking £22 million from them in 1964/5.

After a General Election in which he demonstrated unprecedented mastery of television by a politician, Harold Wilson became Premier. Meanwhile, Mods and Rockers rioted at the seaside, and pirate radio ships stole audiences from the BBC.

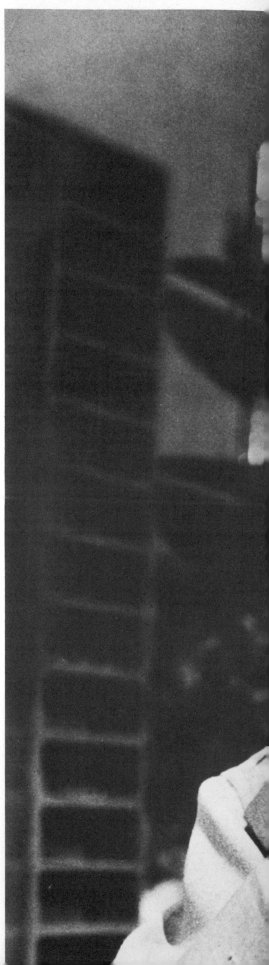

Crossroads, set in a country motel and starring Noele Gordon, was a Midlands triumph. Although it was shown four days a week in the area, it did not achieve national networking until 1972. (ATV)

As Martin Luther King led civil rights marches in America, and won a Nobel Peace Prize, ITV screened a programme of negro protest songs called **Freedom Road,** which won all three major prizes at Berlin's Television Festival. (Associated-Rediffusion)

Sir Kenneth Clark toured **Great Temples of the World** and talked compellingly about both their architectural merits and history. He is seen here at Karnak. (ATV)

To mark Britain's celebration of the 400th anniversary of Shakespeare's birth, ITV showed a production of **A Midsummer Night's Dream.** (Rediffusion)

The face of the year was that of top model Jean Shrimpton. **A World in Action** camera crew trailed her on modelling assignments in New York and London for **The Face On the Cover.** (Granada)

Blackburn's Valerie Martin won the first Miss TVTimes contest, beating 5,000 contestants to take the crown in the final programme, **Glamour All the Way.** Adam Faith sang on the show and Patrick Macnee was one of the panel of star judges. (ABC)

Recalling memories of Will Hay's vintage comedy films, **Fire Crackers** concerned the antics of Cropper's End Fire Brigade and their circa 1907 fire appliance. (ATV)

Blithe Spirit, one of the series **A Choice of Coward,** starred Hattie Jacques as the medium, Madame Arcati, Joanna Dunham as the lovely, spectral Elvira. (Granada)

Derek Granger took over as presenter of **Cinema** from Bamber Gascoigne, who had launched this series of clips from films, and star interviews, three months earlier. (Granada)

With concern growing about the mounting number of accidents on the roads, **This Week** showed a shock programme in which Desmond Wilcox spoke to motorists as they left public houses. (Rediffusion)

The Other Man, by Giles Cooper, had a cast of 200 headed by Michael Caine. At 2 hrs. 20 min., it was ITV's longest-ever play. (Granada)

The comedy series **A Little Big Business** concerned a family furniture firm, with David Kossoff and Francis Matthews as argumentative father and son. (Granada)

Ted Willis devised **The Sullavan Brothers,** a series about four young lawyers, and promised: "We shall fire a few salvoes at British justice."(ATV)

The Celebrity Game, summer replacement for **Take Your Pick,** was a quiz in which contestants guessed celebrities' views on topical subjects. Among the guests was Groucho Marx. (Rediffusion)

Lynn Davies' wir
leap in the long
was amon
highlights of the T
Olympics, broug
British viewe
radio link and sate

Song and dance girl Millicent Martin presented her own series, **Mainly Millicent,** and was the Guild of Television Producers and Directors' Light Entertainment Personality of the Year. Patrick Wymark won the Best Actor award, and Rex Firkin the producer's award, for **The Plane Makers.** Popular American imports included **Burke's Law** and **The Beverly Hillbillies.** ITV initiated schools programmes for infants.

Lord Boothby was among those who discussed topical subjects in **After Dinner.** The series was recorded by concealed cameras to avoid inhibiting the conversation. Andrew Faulds, later a Labour MP, starred in a crime series, **The Protectors,** Edwin Richfield in **It's Dark Outside,** and Alfie Bass and Bill Fraser in the comedy series, **Foreign Affairs.** Eamonn Andrews joined ITV from the BBC on a three-year contract. His first assignment was as host to a variety of well-known guests in the pioneering programme **The Eamonn Andrews Show.**

1965

ITV celebrated the beginning of its second decade with a dinner at London's Guildhall, at which Prime Minister Harold Wilson said: "Independent television has become part of our national anatomy. More than that, it has become part of our social system and part of our national way of life."

Sir Winston Churchill, another British institution, died, and his majestic state funeral was watched by 350 million via Eurovision.

Edward Heath succeeded Sir Alec Douglas-Home as the new Tory leader. Cigarette commercials were banned on ITV as part of an anti-smoking campaign, which resulted in an £8 million-a-year loss of advertising revenue. The combined television and radio licence went up by £1 to £5.

The ITA began consultations with producers, writers and script editors about current output and to exchange ideas for the future.

ITV's documentary approach to the five-hour, live outside broadcast of Sir Winston Churchill's funeral included commentary by Brian Connell, narration by Sir Laurence Olivier, Joseph C. Harsch and Paul Scofield. An edited version, called **The Valiant Man,** was transmitted later.

1965

Redcap introduced a new-style detective: John Thaw as a tough sergeant in the Royal Military Police Special Investigation Branch, whose role was to fight crime in the Army. (ABC)

Front Page Story was made by Rex Firkin and Wilfred Greatorex, producer and script editor of **The Power Game**. This newspaper series had the underlying theme of the individual battling against his persecutors. (ATV)

John Wilder, the ruthless politician of the boardroom in **The Plane Makers**, came back to the screen in **The Power Game**. Now knighted and a merchant banker, he was again played by Patrick Wymark, with Barbara Murray as Lady Wilder. (ATV)

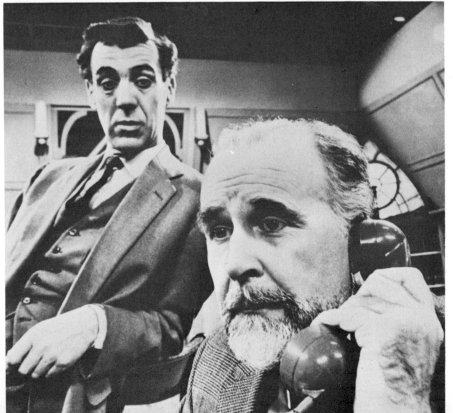

The intelligence agents played by Michael Aldridge and Richard Vernon used their intellectual powers to solve security problems in **The Man in Room 17**. (Granada)

The Successor, a **Play of the Week,** was about a conclave of cardinals choosing a new Pope. Rupert Davies–formerly TV's **Maigret**–beat the typecasting problem to play the Pope. (Anglia)

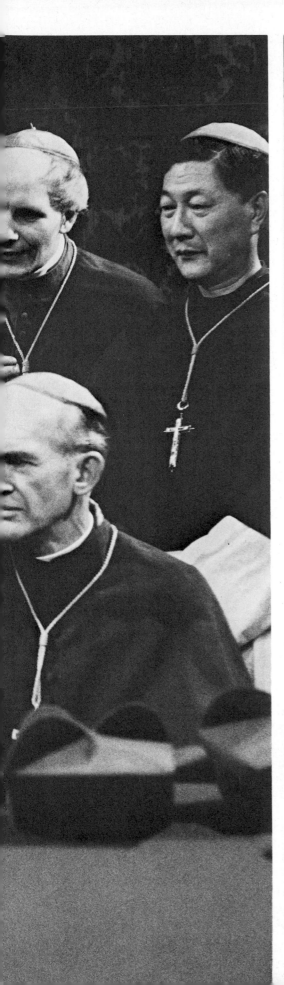

Two lusty Jacobean plays were presented under the title **Blood and Thunder.** Diana Rigg and Gene Anderson starred in Thomas Middleton's **Women Beware Women.** (Granada.)

Following the **Golden Hour** programmes of music and ballet came **Golden Drama,** a two-hour production from a London theatre, in which 30 actors presented dramatic excerpts. Included was Peter O'Toole with soliloquies from **Hamlet.** (ATV)

113

1965

Saturday afternoons became synonymous with sport when ITV launched **World of Sport**, introduced by Eamonn Andrews.

An international quartet of detectives fought criminals against a glamorous South of France background in **Riviera Police.** (Rediffusion)

Thunderbirds, a sophisticated puppet series about an international rescue organisation, was backed by a massive merchandising of toys and comics based on characters such as Lady Penelope and her chauffeur, Parker. (ATV)

Crime in war was the theme of the drama series **Court Martial.** In a bid for sales in the U.S., the two lawyer officers were Americans, played by Bradford Dillman and Peter Graves. (ATV)

1965

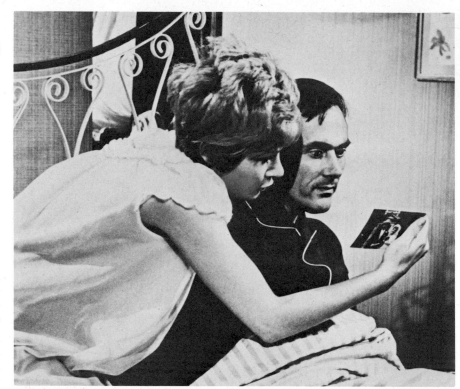

Blackmail–for money, power or love–was among the increasing number of anthology drama series. Dudley Foster and Ann Bell were the stars of this one, **First Offender.** (Rediffusion)

David Kossoff used his own words to tell children stories from the Old Testament in the Sunday series, **Storytime.** (ATV)

Public Eye explored new ground, introducing Alfred Burke as a believable private investigator who never used a gun or met big-time criminals. (ABC)

The Variety Club's ITV
personality of the year
was Bernard Braden,
who also won a
Television Society
silver medal for
On the Braden Beat.
The Variety Club's
showbusiness
personalities of the
year were Morecambe
and Wise, while
Jimmy Tarbuck was
voted the most
promising newcomer.
The Screen Writers'
Guild voted **The Plane
Makers** the best
television series.
The Queen's 10-day
State visit to West
Germany was brought
to the ITV screen live
via Eurovision.
Mr. Swindley, played
in **Coronation Street**
by Arthur Lowe,
achieved a series of
his own – as assistant
manager of a store in
Pardon the Expression.
Diana Rigg joined
The Avengers as the
widowed Emma Peel,
a replacement for
Honor Blackman's
Cathy Gale.
A new American
series was **Peyton Place,**
with Mia Farrow
and Ryan O'Neal.

1966

Continuing uncertainty about the future of British television, in particular the allocation of a fourth channel and the timing of the conversion from 405 lines to 625, caused the ITA to extend existing programme company contracts to 1968.

It then announced that the number of major companies would be increased from four to five in 1968. To make the division of the London area more equal, the weekend company would take over at 7.0 pm on Friday instead of on Saturday morning.

A General Election decided that Harold Wilson should stay at No. 10, and he had a dramatic but fruitless meeting on HMS Tiger with breakaway Rhodesia's leader, Ian Smith. England won the World Cup, beating West Germany 4–2.

A proposal that television cameras should be allowed experimentally into the House of Commons was defeated by one vote.

David Frost began a twice-weekly **Frost Programme,** in which he interviewed well-known people – from Mick Jagger to Frank Cousins. Audience contributions were "orchestrated"– Frost's description of the skilful way he stimulated the debate. (Rediffusion)

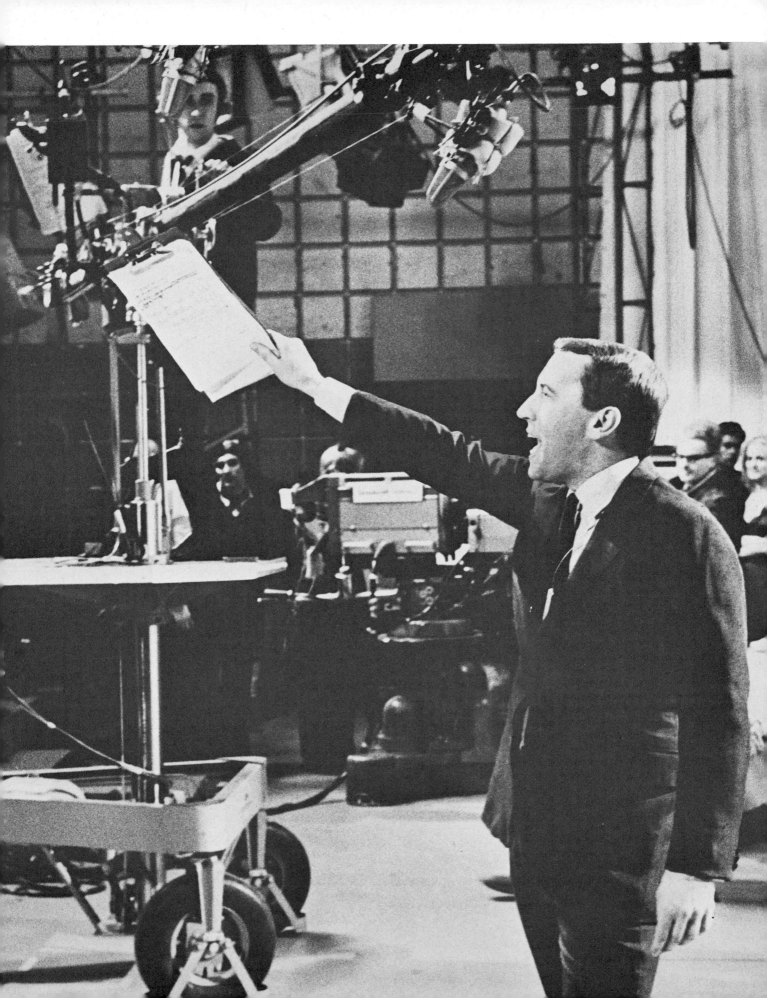

The drama series **Mrs. Thursday** starred Kathleen Harrison as a charlady who inherited a fortune. Creator Lord Ted Willis claimed that it took just 20 seconds to sell the idea to Lew (later Sir Lew) Grade. (ATV)

Intrigue examined the topical subject of industrial espionage, and starred Edward Judd as the counter-agent. (ABC)

Weavers Green was a twice-weekly look at life in a Norfolk village (Anglia)

Steve Forrest played a jet-age dealer in antiques in **The Baron,** a series based on a character created by John Creasey. (ATV)

1966

Victorian tales of the supernatural were dramatised in the series **Mystery and Imagination.** David Buck appeared as the linking central figure and is seen with Virginia McKenna in **The Phantom Lover.** (ABC)

Who Were the British? set out to trace a pedigree for ancient Britons and was Prof. Glyn Daniel's contribution to the popularisation of archaeology on television. (Anglia)

Presenting a new breed of anti-hero, **The Informer** was a disbarred barrister earning a rich living as a tipster for police and insurance companies. Ian Hendry starred in the title role, with Heather Sears as his wife, and Jean Marsh his mistress. (Rediffusion)

A thriller series for
children, **Orlando**
followed the daring
adventures of a
smuggler, played by
Sam Kydd, who had
first appeared in the
adult series, **Crane.**
(Rediffusion)

George and the Dragon starred the new situation comedy team of Sidney James and Peggy Mount, who played handyman and housekeeper in a stately home. (ATV)

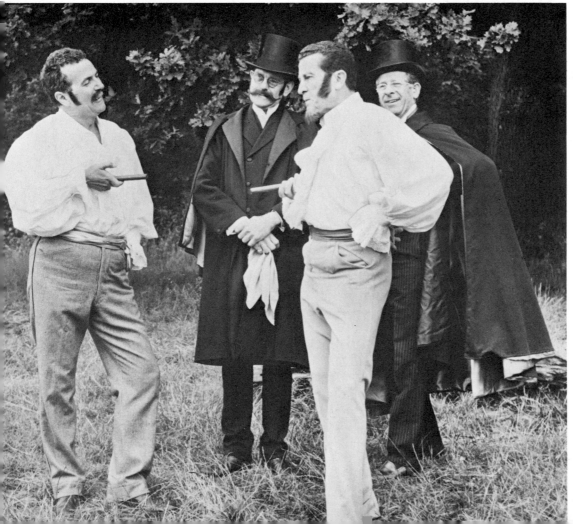

All Square explored Michael Bentine's inimitable brand of comedy. This zany series found humour in everything from duelling to the esoteric sport of dwile-flonking. (ATV)

1966

The Stories of D.H. Lawrence, mainly about Nottinghamshire mining villages, were adapted into a drama series that kept faithfully to the spirit of the original. (Granada)

Terence Rattigan's Nelson – A Study in Miniature, with Michael Bryant as the Admiral, was written at the suggestion of Prince Philip, who later introduced the play on screen. (ATV)

England, led by Bobby Moore, achieved a memorable victory in The World Cup. ITV's nightly coverage of games throughout England was presented by Eamonn Andrews.

Alastair Burnet introduced ITN's second General Election programme in 11 months, and won the Guild of Television Producers and Directors' Richard Dimbleby award. Geoffrey Cox, Editor of ITN, was knighted. The Variety Club of Great Britain made a special double award to Hughie Green, of **Double Your Money**, and **Take Your Pick's** Michael Miles for the continuing popularity of their programmes. Green took his **Double Your Money** team to Russia to stage a programme with Muscovite contestants.

Danger Man, starring Patrick McGoohan, won a Hollywood Screen Producers' Guild award for the best-produced TV programme.

A craze for **Batman**, the pre-war strip cartoon for children, brought an American television series, with Adam West as the caped crusader. Documentary producer Adrian Cowell and cameraman Chris Menges returned from their travels in Thailand, Tibet, Laos and Burma with two highly praised programmes, **Light of Asia** and **The Opium Trail**.

1967

The ITA invited franchise applications for the new contract period beginning in 1968, and many strangely named consortia were formed to bid for them. There was a total of 36 applications from 16 new groups and the 14 existing companies.

ITA Chairman Lord Hill announced the successful organisations in June, after which Prime Minister Wilson–in a surprise and controversial decision–moved him to the Chairmanship of the BBC.

BBC2 was allowed to go into colour on 625 lines UHF; ITV was also making programmes in colour but they were shown in black and white. The colour was seen only in America and other countries to which the programmes were sold.

ITN launched **News at Ten,** the first regular half-hour news on a major channel. Within days it was an established success after showing exciting film of Col. Colin Mitchell leading his Highlanders in the re-taking of the Crater district of Aden.

Israel mauled the Arabs in the Six Day War and the revolutionary Che Guevara was killed in Bolivia. Dr. Christian Barnard performed his first heart transplant. Jeremy Thorpe succeeded Jo Grimond as Liberal leader, and the BBC introduced a pop radio channel and the first local radio.

News at Ten combined news and analysis in a programme twice the length of the bulletin it replaced. The new format introduced a two-man newscaster system enabling late items to be fed to the man off-camera. (ITN)

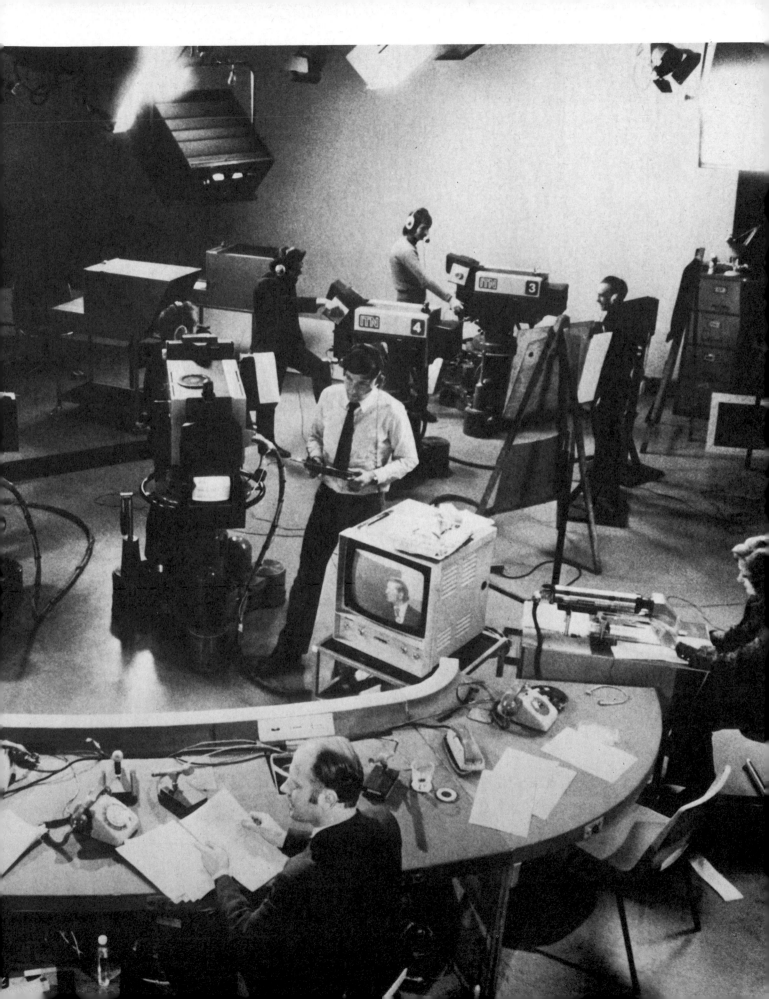

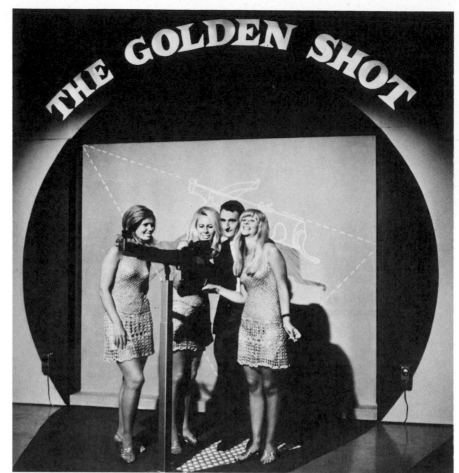

THE GOLDEN SHOT

The Golden Shot was a new type of TV game in which the contestants fired bolts from an electronic bow at novelty targets. Jackie Rae was first compere. (ATV)

At Last the 1948 Show set a new trend, with John Cleese, Tim Brooke-Taylor and Graham Chapman exploring the type of lunatic comedy that would lead to **Monty Python's Flying Circus** and **The Goodies.** It also starred lovely Aimi Macdonald in a dumb blonde role. (Rediffusion)

Television created
a new sport in
rallycross. Devised
specially for
World of Sport by
director Robert
Reid, it featured
saloon cars in
events combining
road and rough
country racing. (ABC)

Adapted from three
novels by Phyllis
Bentley, **Inheritance**
related the saga
of a Yorkshire mill
family from 1812
to 1965. The main
actors played
several generations
of the Oldroyd
family. (Granada)

Ronnie Corbett portrayed a dithery, tongue-tied little man in a comedy series about life in suburbia, **No, That's Me Over Here.** (Rediffusion)

Richard Bradford was McGill in **Man In a Suitcase.** A bounty hunter, always on the move, he typified the rugged hero of the Sixties. (ATV)

Callan, a series developed from a play about a licensed-to-kill British agent, created a hero to rank among TV's all-time greats. It made Edward Woodward one of Britain's most popular actors, and eventually won a Writers' Guild award for creator James Mitchell. (ABC)

Featured in **The Odd Man** and **It's Dark Outside,** Chief Insp. Rose (William Mervyn) won his own series, **Mr. Rose,** in which he had retired to write his memoirs. (Granada)

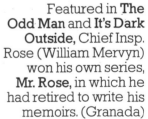

One of the most extensive open air sets ever built for a TV drama was constructed at Elstree for **Market in Honey Lane,** a series about a London street market, its stallholders and customers. (ATV)

The Prisoner was an imaginative series concerning the mind-bending, will-sapping treatment meted out to a former British agent. Patrick McGoohan was deviser, producer and star and also wrote, directed and edited some of the episodes. (ATV)

Acclaimed many times as a new star, Des O'Connor finally proved his potential as a dollar earner when **The Des O'Connor Show** was exported to America. (ATV)

Tonight with Dave Allen was described as a "late night miscellany". The Irish comedian conducted interviews and risked his neck in many strange stunts. (ATV)

More than 20 million viewers watched the marriage of Elsie Tanner and Steve Tanner in **Coronation Street**, Britain's top serial. (Granada)

Pudgy comedian Joe Baker so impressed an ATV staff party at which he performed that he was given his own TV series, **My Man Joe.** (ATV)

John Bluthal
Joe Lynch starre
Never Mind
Quality, Fee
Width, a com
series about an I
Jewish tailo
partnership.(A

Prince Philip introduced **The Enchanted Isles**, a programme about the wildlife of the Galapagos in the Pacific. It won awards in Monte Carlo and America. Comedy actors given series during the year included Arthur Lowe, (**Turn Out the Lights**); Harry H. Corbett, (**Mr. Aitch**); and Joe Baker (**My Man Joe**). Children's series included **The Lion, the Witch and the Wardrobe**, the C. S. Lewis allegory, **The Flower of Gloster**, about children on a narrow boat traversing canals from North Wales to London; and **Sexton Blake**, the adventures of the enduring detective.

1968

The new ITV companies began operating in July. Among them were Yorkshire, whose founders included Alan Whicker, London Weekend (David Frost), Harlech (Richard Burton) and Thames, which was a merger of ABC and Rediffusion.

Simultaneously, a new TVTimes with regional editions was launched to replace separate programme journals. Favourite programmes, such as **Double Your Money** and **Take Your Pick,** were discontinued and new ones introduced in sweeping changes. The BBC competed strenuously for the mass audience by scheduling new series of popular programmes at peak times on its major channel.

Russian tanks invaded Czechoslovakia to smash Alexander Dubcek's liberalising regime. Pictures of students shouting defiance at the Russians were transmitted live by Czech television before it was shut down, and relayed via Eurovision.

Elsewhere in a violent year, Martin Luther King and Robert Kennedy were assassinated and there were civil rights demonstrations in Londonderry. Richard Nixon became America's President.

While educationists argued the merits of comprehensive and grammar schools, **Please Sir!** won laughs with the story of a recently qualified teacher in a tough secondary school. As the harassed master, John Alderton won the Royal Television Society's award for "outstanding male personality". (LWT)

1968

We Have Ways of **Making You Laugh** was the challenging title Frank Muir chose for one of the first programmes resulting from his appointment as head of light entertainment with one of the new companies. He also starred in the show. (LWT)

One of many ideas from Lord Ted Willis, **Virgin of the Secret Service** was a spoof spy series concerning an early secret agent, Capt. Robert Virgin, who travelled the Empire in the early 1900s. (ATV)

Black Power salutes
at the Mexico
Olympic Games,
which were televised
live via satellite
and Eurovision.

1968

Vince Powell and Harry Driver created some of the most popular comedy series of the Sixties. **Nearest and Dearest** teamed Hylda Baker and Jimmy Jewel as a brother and sister who inherited a run-down pickle business. (Granada)

Children were given an insight into the period of World War One through **Tom Grattan's War,** the story of a boy living in that era. (Yorkshire)

Frontier looked at
the theme of British
Imperial history –
little explored at
this time – for a
drama series about
soldiers on the
North West Frontier
of India. (Thames)

Established by **The Power Game** as one of Britain's top TV actors, Patrick Wymark was invited to choose four **Playhouse** productions in which he would like to star. Among his choices was August Strindberg's **The Father.** (ATV)

Do Not Adjust Your Set was a trend-setting series for children which won a Prix Jeunesse first prize at Munich. (Rediffusion)

A new-style TVTimes, reflecting the changed image of ITV, was introduced in September. Its 13 regional editions replaced existing ITV programme journals produced by a number of publishers.

Patrick Cargill was the endearing head of the Glover family in **Father, Dear Father,** the story of a divorcee's bid to rear two nubile daughters. (Thames)

145

A master criminal's bid for world domination was the exciting theme of **Freewheelers,** a series aimed at teenagers. (Southern)

A Man Of Our Times was a dramatic examination of the prototypal modern man and his ambitions and fears. The role was played by George Cole. (Rediffusion)

Horrifying film from Nigeria showed the execution of an officer for his part in the murder of Biafrans. (ITN)

Linda Thorson
succeeded Diana
Rigg as Patrick
Macnee's partner in
The Avengers.
Nemone Lethbridge
wrote **The Franchise
Trail,** a play that
satirised the rush
for ITV contracts.
David Frost introduced
everything from
interviews to variety
in his three weekly
programmes. Two of
his "confrontations"
with subjects who
were later arrested
led to an outcry about
"trial by television."
The video disc was
used to provide
instant replays
in sporting events.
A £5 supplementary
licence for colour TV
was introduced; a
colour licence cost £10.

1969

The year of colour for ITV and BBC1. Lord Aylestone –who succeeded Lord Hill as chairman of the ITA – performed ITV's switch-on ceremony.

Otherwise, it was a year of consolidation as ITV overcame the difficulties that had followed its reconstruction. The collapse of the Emley Moor transmitter mast in Yorkshire did not help, but ITV re-established itself in the ratings as the most popular channel.

And on one of the most memorable nights in history, the night when man landed on the Moon, professional critics and viewers agreed that ITV's 15-hour presentation was superior to that of the BBC.

The cost of television licences rose by £1–to £6 for black and white sets and £11 for colour. But the number of colour sets increased from 100,000 to 270,000.

President de Gaulle resigned. Prime Minister Wilson sent an invasion force to the island of Anguilla, where a self-appointed President was demanding independence. The voting age was reduced from 21 to 18, and the Open University was founded.

Man On the Moon was ITV's longest-ever production–from 6.0pm on July 20 to 9.0 the following morning. News and comment on the Moon mission alternated with David Frost's gala variety show and phone-in session. Alastair Burnet headed ITN's team in the "Moon studio", with comment from TVTimes Science Editor Peter Fairley.

1969

The Dustbinmen, Jack Rosenthal's comedy series about the crew of a dustcart known as Thunderbird Three, achieved the unusual distinction of reaching No. One in the JICTAR ratings with each of its six episodes. (Granada)

Three of the most talented producers and directors of the BBC's **Wednesday Play** series – Tony Garnett, Kenith Trodd and James McTaggart – formed their own company, Kestrel Productions, to make plays for ITV. One of the most successful was **Bangelstein's Boys,** the story of a rugby club's weekend excursion. (LWT)

Continuing the role he had created in **Gazette,** Gerald Harper starred as **Hadleigh,** the smooth Yorkshire landowner who was to become one of the most popular characters on ITV. (Yorkshire)

The Mind of Mr. J. G. Reeder starred Hugh Burden as Edgar Wallace's mild-mannered detective with an intuitive understanding of the criminal's devious intellect. (Thames)

Stars on Sunday was the first religious series to enter the Top 20 viewing figures. This was achieved by mixing actors and pop stars, prelates and politicians in lavish settings, to sing, or read verses from the Bible. (Yorkshire)

Doctor in the House was another comedy series which was to receive popular acclaim. Based on Richard Gordon's novels about young medical men, it developed its theme through 138 episodes and over more than five years. (LWT)

The comedy series **On the Buses** made its debut, with Reg Varney as the genial bus driver. A year later, Sun readers were to vote it their "top series". (LWT)

The Gold Robbers was a skilfully made drama series about the detective work carried out by a dedicated policeman (played by Peter Vaughan), following a massive bullion theft. (LWT)

Instead of writing a book, Lord Louis Mountbatten chose to present his memoirs on ITV. **The Life and Times of Lord Mountbatten,** filmed around the world, won Producer Peter Morley a Royal Television Society silver medal. An S.F.T.A. award for best script went to historian John Terraine. (Thames)

Rodney Bewes was co-writer, co-producer and star of **Dear Mother ...Love Albert**. This comedy series hinged on the lively letters a young man sent home to his mother (Thames)

Special Branch saw the debut of a new-style police investigator. Derren Nesbitt played Det.-Chief Insp. Jordan as a fashionable dresser, with floral shirts, wide ties and flared trousers. (Thames)

A new character to replace John Wilder, the ruthless businessman played by Patrick Wymark in **The Power Game,** arrived with the creation of David Main in **The Main Chance.** John Stride starred as the tough, ambitious young solicitor. (Yorkshire)

Eamonn Andrews revived his biographical show, **This is Your Life,** which he had presented on BBC Television from 1953 to 1964. Andrews' faith was justified and it was soon the most popular show in Britain. (Thames)

The Investiture of Prince Charles as Prince of Wales was a day of pageantry at Caernarvon Castle. ITV's commentators were Brian Connell and Wynford Vaughan-Thomas, and the stirring tribute to Wales was read by actor Richard Burton.

A gambling innovation was the introduction of **The ITV Seven.** Viewers placed accumulator bets covering seven races from two meetings shown in **World of Sport.** The advantage was that punters were eligible for a proportion of their winnings even if only five or six consecutive selections won.

ITN set out to discover the truth about Loch Ness Monster stories and mounted a big expedition involving a midget submarine and echo sounders. But the Monster failed to appear before the waiting cameras.

Ronnie Barker, who appeared as a doddering peer named Lord Rustless in **Hark at Barker,** was the Variety Club's choice as ITV Personality of the Year. But TVTimes readers voted Tom Jones top of their poll.

Male of the Species, a trilogy of plays by Alun Owen, was introduced by Laurence Olivier and starred Sean Connery, Michael Caine and Paul Scofield. An unknown, Anna Calder-Marshall, who co-starred in all three, won an Emmy award.

Royal Family, the most human look yet at the Queen and her family, was a 115-minute documentary made by a joint BBC/ITV consortium.

157

1970

Sir Robert Fraser, Director General of the ITA since its inception, and chief architect of ITV's federal structure, retired at the age of 66. He said that the most significant development of the past 15 years had been "the growth of TV as a medium of information alongside TV as a medium of entertainment, which it was—almost pure and simple—in 1955. Now it is theatre and newspaper in one—a pregnant social change."

The events of the year, in which Edward Heath became Premier, underlined Sir Robert's words. On Budget Day, there was an explosion on board Apollo 13 as it journeyed towards the Moon. Alastair Burnet—ITV's man for big occasions—fronted a combined Budget and Apollo programme that continued until 4am when the astronauts were out of danger.

And ITN gained a world scoop with exclusive film of the blowing up by Palestinian guerillas of three airliners they had hijacked to Jordan.

But ITV's profits dropped to their lowest level for a decade, due largely to the increased costs of colour transmissions and the fact that the companies charged no premium for commercials in colour.

The longest, costliest ITV drama series to date was **A Family at War.** Created by John Finch, it told the story of a Liverpool family at war within itself and was set in the framework of World War Two. (Granada)

Manhunt, a serial about a French Resistance girl and an RAF pilot on the run through occupied France, featured Alfred Lynch, Peter Barkworth and beautiful discovery Cyd Hayman. (LWT)

Phyllis Calvert, former star of British films, became a star of television as **Kate**, a magazine columnist answering readers' personal problems. (Yorkshire)

The expert and forthright views of ITV's World Cup panel – Bob McNab, Pat Crerand, Derek Dougan and Malcolm Allison, encouraged by presenters Jimmy Hill and Brian Moore – rivalled the football itself. England were eliminated in the quarter finals.

161

1970

The Lovers, a comedy series about an attractive but ingenuous courting couple – played by Paula Wilcox and Richard Beckinsale – won a Writers' Guild award for Geoffrey Lancashire and Jack Rosenthal. (Granada)

Crime of Passion, a series of fictional murder trials set in a French court, was the creation of Lord Ted Willis. (ATV)

Romance among old age pensioners sounded an unpromising subject for comedy, but Irene Handl and Wilfred Pickles gave **For the Love of Ada** wide appeal. (Thames)

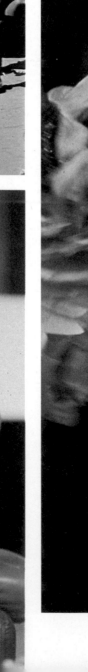

Adrian Cowell, an independent producer specialising in programmes from remote places, went to the Amazon jungle of Brazil to make **The Tribe That Hides From Man,** which won a Prix Italia award, and a silver medal at the Venice Film Festival. (ATV)

Humphrey Burton edited and presented **Aquarius,** a major new arts programme which was shown at first fortnightly, later weekly. (LWT)

164

Simon Dee, once a disc jockey on a pirate radio ship, became host of an entertaining new chat show. The series was ended after he quarrelled with executives over choice of guests. (LWT)

Alan Whicker roved the world interviewing a rich variety of subjects–ranging from Francois (Papa Doc) Duvalier, the dictator of Haiti, to the Bluebell dancers of Paris. (Yorkshire)

1970

One of the answers to a plea from the ITA for more imaginative series for children was **Catweazle,** in which an 11th century magician found himself transported to modern England. (LWT)

Charlie Nairn and his television team lived for five weeks among South American Indians to film **A Clearing in the Jungle** for an occasional series, **The Disappearing World.** (Granada)

Because all scheduled flights in and out of Jordan had been cancelled, ITN chartered a 120-seat airliner to fly out exclusive film of the destruction of hijacked jets on Dawson's Field. (ITN)

In the six-part documentary series **The Day Before Yesterday,** producer Phillip Whitehead – later to become a Labour MP – examined the period 1945 to 1963 with the help of people who shaped the history of those years.

Ronald Fraser starred as Badger in **The Misfit,** the comic misadventures of an Englishman who returned from the Colonies to a vastly changed Britain. The series won Roy Clarke a Writers' Guild award.

Coronation Street reached its 1,000th episode and received the Sun newspaper's "top series" award.

Singer/actor Tommy Steele was one of the stars in ITV's lively production of **Twelfth Night.**

167

1971

Chancellor of the Exchequer Anthony Barber eased the credit squeeze in a July mini-Budget and the hire purchase of colour television sets rocketed. Manufacturers could not meet the demand and had to ration supplies to shops, where prices were now displayed in decimal currency.

Within a year, a million new colour sets had been licensed, in spite of a £1 increase in licence fees – to £7 for black and white and £12 for colour.

A £10 million reduction in the levy on ITV's advertising income also encouraged the television industry. Some other concerns had a less cheerful year: Rolls-Royce and Upper Clyde Shipbuilders went into liquidation and the Daily Sketch ceased publication.

There were troubles at London Weekend Television, where financial problems had hindered the company from fulfilling its original programme plans, and a number of key executives resigned.

The troubles ended after newspaper owner Rupert Murdoch took a financial stake in the company and John Freeman, former British Ambassador to the U.S., and a noted television broadcaster, was appointed chairman and chief executive.

A saga that was to run for five years and 68 episodes, **Upstairs, Downstairs** began the dramatic story of the Bellamy family and their servants in the Edwardian era. The programme was voted Best Drama Series by the Society of Film and Television Arts. (LWT)

Former pop singer
Adam Faith emerged
as an actor of charm
in **Budgie,** the story of
an unsuccessful crook
in seedy Soho. (LWT)

A television team accompanied Chris Bonington on his successful assault on the previously unscaled South Face of Annapurna in the Himalayas for **The Hardest Way Up.** (Thames)

Moving on from the politics, diplomacy and money of **The Power Game,** Wilfred Greatorex created **Hine,** about the manoeuvring and money of an international arms dealer, played by Barrie Ingham. (ATV)

Persuasion was an elegant, five-part series based on Jane Austen's posthumously published novel about lost love reborn. (Granada)

The unusual casting of American Richard Chamberlain – formerly television's Dr. Kildare – as **Hamlet** attracted a wide audience for this two-hour Shakespearian production. (ATV)

After three years on BBC Television in **Not In Front of the Children,** Wendy Craig moved to ITV to play a similarly scatterbrained role, appearing as a widow with two children in **...And Mother Makes Three.** (Thames)

America's Tony Curtis and Britain's Roger Moore were teamed in **The Persuaders,** a slick action series and one of the shows that helped ATV win a third Queen's Award to Industry for overseas sales. (ATV)

The Comedians used six or eight stand-up comics per show and edited their gags into a succession of non-stop laughs. The programme's new approach made stars of little known comedians. (Granada)

With the teaming of stars as important as the storyline in situation comedy, **Bless This House** created a winning combination –Sidney James and Diana Coupland as husband and wife, with Sally Geeson and Robin Stewart as their children. (Thames)

The Fenn Street Gang, sequel to **Please Sir!** traced the adventures of Form 5C's pupils in post-school life. (LWT)

Prince Philip launched a wildlife preservation campaign when he introduced film from Kenya in **Now or Never,** in the **Survival** series. (Anglia)

Lord Snowdon directed his third film, **Born to be Small,** a compassionate documentary about "people of restricted growth". (ATV)

Man at the Top was a series reflecting the permissiveness of the time through the amorous exploits of John Braine's hero, Joe Lampton (played by Kenneth Haigh). (Thames)

ITN celebrated 1,000 editions of **News at Ten,** of which 632 had featured in the Top Twenty.

Prince Andrew and Prince Edward appeared with the Queen in her Christmas Day television broadcast.

The campaign for equal opportunities for women received support from **Justice,** in which Margaret Lockwood played Harriet Peterson, a tough – but attractive – barrister, more than a match for male competition.

A political thriller series, **The Guardians** presented a chilling picture of a Britain in which democracy had been replaced by quasi-military rule.

1972

Restrictions on television hours were swept away by the Government following a long campaign by ITV for more time. Christopher Chataway, the former ITN newscaster, made the announcement as Minister of Posts and Telecommunications. ITV immediately planned up to 20 extra hours of weekday television to provide a total of 105 hours viewing a week. The television day stretched to 15 hours and breakfast time programmes were forecast. In the meantime, new afternoon serials aimed chiefly at women were introduced and ITN added a lunchtime news bulletin. Television news covered many big stories during the year. Thirteen were shot dead in Londonderry when troops ended an illegal march. Arab guerillas murdered two members of the Israeli team in the Olympic village in Munich; later, nine hostages were killed when the terrorists were ambushed.

A state of emergency followed a strike by miners and brought severe restrictions on the use of electricity. The ITA became the Independent Broadcasting Authority (IBA) when it also assumed responsibility for proposed independent radio stations.

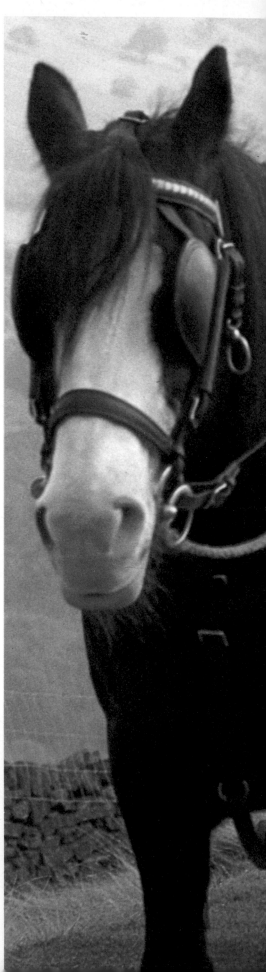

Country Matters,
based on short stories
by H. E. Bates and
A. E. Coppard,
brought new stature to
the anthology drama
series; the Society
of Film and Television
Arts voted it
"Best Drama Series".
(Granada)

Viennese waltzes played by the London Symphony Orchestra added an extra dimension to **The Strauss Family,** eight plays celebrating the 19th century composers. (ATV)

The endless search for new television detectives led to **Van der Valk,** with Barry Foster as the Amsterdam policeman of Nicholas Freeling's books. (Thames)

My Good Woman, an elegant comedy series set in the stockbroker belt, teamed Sylvia Syms, as a charity worker, and Leslie Crowther as her long-suffering husband. (ATV)

Black Beauty, Anna Sewell's classic story for children about a girl and her horse, provided the basis for a drama series. (LWT)

Capitalising on the popularity of impressionists, **Who Do You Do?** featured the best-known in a series of fast-moving, half-hour shows. (LWT)

Sale of the Century, a new quiz show, offered successful contestants the opportunity to acquire expensive products at special bargain prices. (Anglia)

The camp humour of Larry Grayson made him the comic of the year and **Shut That Door!** – the title of his series – a popular catchphrase. (ATV)

Love Thy Neighbour tackled the controversial subject of race relations with shrewd but unbiased good humour. It derived its laughs from the relationship between black and white couples. (Thames)

183

1972

The 24-part **Arthur of the Britons,** with Oliver Tobias playing him as a tribal warlord, was claimed to be the biggest production undertaken by one of ITV's smaller companies. (HTV)

To avoid irritating viewers with duplicate coverage, ITV left live transmission of the Munich Olympics to the BBC and included nightly highlights in news bulletins.

Adam Smith was ITV's first religious drama series made for Sunday evening viewing, and was about a minister in a Scottish country town. (Granada)

Robert Kee presented **First Report**, the new lunchtime news, with a greater degree of freedom than had ever been given to a newscaster. (ITN)

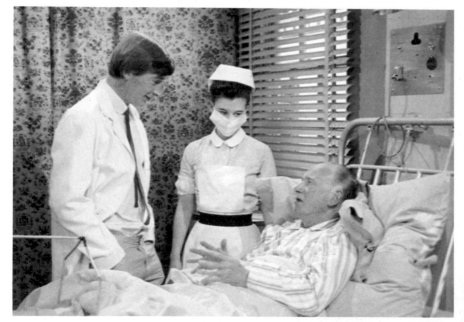

All those viewers – and television executives – who had regretted the ending of **Emergency-Ward 10** in 1967, now welcomed a new serial, **General Hospital**, for afternoon viewing. (ATV)

Another new afternoon serial, made possible by the de-restriction of television hours, was **Emmerdale Farm**, a twice-weekly story about a farming family in the dales. (Yorkshire)

A row broke out when the IBA suggested that a Glyndebourne production of Verdi's opera **Macbeth** should be screened at Christmas; viewers protested that they wanted lighter fare. In the event, the opera was shown on December 27 and was watched by two million – enough to have filled Covent Garden Opera House daily for two years. MP's again barred television cameras from the House of Commons, this time by 26 votes.

Weekend World, a Sunday newspaper of the screen introduced by Peter Jay, made its debut; it was highly praised, although the audience available at 11am on Sundays was small. The programme was subsequently transmitted at 11.30am, then became a regular midday show.

1973

Viewers acclaimed **The World at War,** a massive 26-week production about World War Two, while a ceasefire prevailed in Vietnam. But letter and fire bombs exploded in London, British frigates fended off gunboats in a battle over Iceland's disputed 50-mile fishing limits, and trade unions defied the rulings of the Industrial Relations Court.

Echoes of wartime were evoked by the issue of petrol coupons to motorists in a fuel crisis that followed the raising of oil prices by Middle East producers.

The wedding of the year was that of Princess Anne and Capt. Mark Phillips, who gave television interviews two days before their marriage. The most colourful legal battle of the year concerned **Warhol,** an ITV programme against which Ross McWhirter obtained an injunction on the grounds it constituted an offence against good taste. This was later lifted by the Court of Appeal, which ruled that censorship of ITV programmes was the IBA's job.

A 50-strong team spent nearly four years preparing **The World at War.** A meticulously researched history of World War Two, it won an Emmy award for outstanding documentary treatment. (Thames)

1973

Laurence Olivier – narrator of **The World at War** – won an Emmy award for his performance in Eugene O'Neill's tragic play, **Long Day's Journey Into Night,** performed by the original National Theatre cast. (ATV)

Shabby Tiger was a seven-part adaptation of a Howard Spring novel about a wild Irish girl and her love for an artist. (Granada)

ITV kept pace with developments on the pop music scene with **James Paul McCartney,** in which the ex-Beatle introduced his new group, Wings. (ATV)

It is comparatively rare for a TV series to be built around a woman, but this happened with **Beryl's Lot,** the story of a middle aged char, played by Carmel McSharry. (Yorkshire)

An ITV team went behind the Iron Curtain to film **Olga,** a profile of the 17-year-old Russian gymnast Olga Korbut, whose grace and charm won hearts at the 1972 Olympics. (Granada)

1973

ITV devoted nearly six hours to the wedding of Princess Anne and Capt. Mark Phillips. Twenty-eight camera crews and eight commentators covered the glittering occasion, with Andrew Gardner describing the scene live in Westminster Abbey.

Richard Burton and Elizabeth Taylor – members of the consortium that set up HTV in 1967 – starred in **Divorce His: Divorce Hers,** a two-part drama screened before their marriage hit trouble. (HTV)

The fight of the year and exclusive to ITV – European Heavy-weight Champion Joe Bugner was beaten on points over 12 rounds by Muhammad Ali in Las Vegas. (Independent Television Sport Production)

1973

The Bröntes of Haworth was a dramatic evocation of the lives of the remarkable, novel-writing Brönte sisters – Anne, Emily and Charlotte – and their family. (Yorkshire)

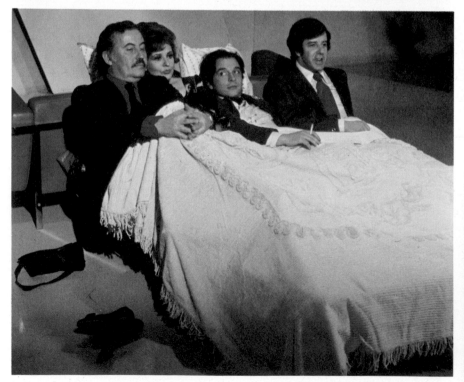

Russell Harty was host of a controversial chat show and won a Pye award as Outstanding New Male TV Personality. Alan Browning, Pat Phoenix and David Bailey joined him on this occasion. (LWT)

In **The Stanley Baxter Big Picture Show,** Baxter's superbly accurate impersonations were superimposed on spectacular settings. He won the S.F.T.A. award for Best Light Entertainment Programme. (LWT)

A new element was brought to television sport with **Indoor League.** Introduced by former England fast bowler Fred Trueman, it featured darts, table skittles, shove ha'penny and American pool. (Yorkshire)

Sam, a new work by John Finch, creator of **A Family at War,** concerned a boy growing up in the impoverished Thirties and was an immediate success. (Granada)

The Death of Adolf Hitler, one of many plays and films in 1973 about the Fuehrer, gave Frank Finlay the opportunity for a memorably ranting performance. (LWT)

Jonathan Dimbleby's **This Week** report from Ethiopia led to £1,500,000 being raised in Britain for famine relief, and won him an award named after his father, Richard Dimbleby. (Thames)

Helen – A Wom
Today was a na
successor to **A
Of Our Ti**
Helen was playe
Alison Fiske in a s
that commente
contemporary m
and marriage. (I

ORACLE, the IBA's system for printing out the latest news and other information on a domestic TV set, was demonstrated for the first time.

London Broadcasting, Britain's first independent radio station, went on the air on October 8. It was followed by Capital on October 16, and Radio Clyde at the end of the year.

Kung Fu became a craze with the showing in some regions of the Hollywood series starring David Carradine as the inscrutable, high-kicking monk, Caine. Veteran comic Jimmy Jewel turned actor for **Spring and Autumn,** a poignant comedy series about the relationship between young and old.

Hunter's Walk, a police series set in the East Midlands, achieved a high degree of realism by concentrating mainly on the solving of small time crime.

Meanwhile, a new series of **Special Branch** introduced new detectives, played by George Sewell and Patrick Mower, and was filmed on location. Transmission of **Warhol,** the David Bailey documentary about the pop artist Andy Warhol, was delayed by a court action. But it was eventually shown to a large audience, most of whom found it boring rather than offensive, according to an IBA survey.

1974

The television year began with a 10.30pm curfew, which was imposed by the Government – along with a three-day working week – following industrial action by miners, power engineers and train drivers. The curfew ended after a General Election in February. Although this produced no overall majority in Parliament, Edward Heath yielded No. 10 to Harold Wilson and, in a November election, Labour won an overall majority.

The setting up by the new Government of the Committee on the Future of Broadcasting, under Lord Annan, left television's long-term future unpredictable. However, the immediate life of the ITV companies (due for a review of contracts in 1976) was extended by a further three years.

When Turkish paratroopers invaded Cyprus, ITN's Michael Nicholson gained a world scoop by being on the spot to interview them. Princess Anne escaped a kidnap attempt. President Nixon resigned in the aftermath of the Watergate scandal.

Churchill Centenary Year was marked by a distinguished drama series in which Lee Remick played the dazzling **Jennie, Lady Randolph Churchill.** (Thames)

1974

The Royal Shakespeare Company's two-and-a-half-hour production of **Antony and Cleopatra,** with Richard Johnson and Janet Suzman, was voted Best Play of the Year by the Society of Film and Television Arts.

Intimate Strangers was another dramatic examination of middle class marriage and morality from Richard Bates, producer of **A Man Of Our Times** and **Helen – A Woman of Today.** (LWT)

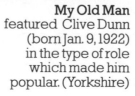

My Old Man featured Clive Dunn (born Jan. 9, 1922) in the type of role which made him popular. (Yorkshire)

Dick Clement and
Ian La Frenais were
the most acclaimed
comedy scriptwriters
of the year. In their
Thick as Thieves,
Bob Hoskins was a
released prisoner
who found his wife
(Pat Ashton) sharing
the home with
his friend, played
by John Thaw. (LWT)

The Inheritors, a
drama series on the
topical theme of an
ancient family estate
being broken-up,
starred Peter Egan
and Robert
Urquhart (HTV)

In **Napoleon and Love,** a major historical drama series by Philip Mackie, Ian Holm played the Emperor and Billie Whitelaw was Josephine. (Thames)

Set in the 19th century, **Boy Dominic** – a "family serial" for Sunday afternoons – followed the adventures of a 12-year-old seeking his shipwrecked father. (Yorkshire)

Kenneth More justified his surprise casting as G.K. Chesterton's **Father Brown**. Angela Douglas (Mrs. More) also appeared in the series. (ATV)

Norman Wisdom returned for his second ITV comedy series, **A Little Bit of Wisdom.** (ATV)

John Mills and Lilli Palmer were among the international stars in **The Zoo Gang,** Paul Gallico's stories about French Resistance workers after the war. (ATV)

South Riding, based on Winifred Holtby's 1936 novel, was voted the Society of Film and Television Arts' Best Drama Series. Dorothy Tutin starred. (Yorkshire)

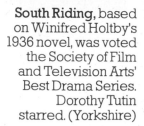

Sunley's Daughter traced the hardships endured by Joe Sunley and his daughter on their Yorkshire Moors farm, where they bred the much sought after Cleveland Bay horses. (Yorkshire)

A new scriptwriting team was acclaimed when playwrights Julia Jones and Donald Churchill joined forces to create **Moody and Pegg,** with Judy Cornwell and Derek Waring in the title roles. (Thames)

Richard Beckinsale as student lodger, Leonard Rossiter as grasping landlord, in the comedy series **Rising Damp.** (Yorkshire)

The contemporary popularity of working men's clubs was reflected by one specially created for television, **Wheeltappers and Shunters Social Club.** (Granada)

Following **The Julie Andrews Hour,** a series which won seven Emmy Awards and the Silver Rose of Montreux in 1973, she starred in five one-hour spectaculars, including **Julie on Sesame Street.** (ATV)

For ITN's General Election coverage, a machine used for planning knitting patterns was coupled to the programme's computer. It printed out results and forecasts in instant diagrams.

"Open access" programmes, providing television time for organisations and pressure groups to present their views, were introduced in many regions.

The Prison, screened as the first **Armchair Cinema** presentation, was among Britain's earliest 90-minute, made-for-television films.

Peter Jay, of **Weekend World,** was the Royal Television Society's Personality of the Year. John Pilger introduced his own current affairs series during **Weekend World's** summer break.

Video cassette recorders became available for home use. Prized status symbols, at more than £400 they were £100 dearer than a colour set.

The House of Commons again barred television cameras–this time by 25 votes.

1975

It was **Edward the Seventh**'s year. This distinguished 13-part series was a glorious success; in part, perhaps, because of the contrast between its elegant portrayal of a bygone era and the violence of 1975.

South Vietnam fell to the Vietcong, Irish bombs exploded in London's West End, and 41 people died in London Underground's worst crash. Dissension about the Common Market led to Britain's first national referendum. There was rampaging inflation, and television licences were among the items that became dearer – £18 for colour and £8 for black and white. Meanwhile, ITV companies, which do not benefit from licence revenue, complained about rising costs.

Mrs. Thatcher became leader of the Conservative party and Lady Plowden Chairman of the IBA. With Sir Michael Swann already at the BBC, both networks were now headed by educationists.

Proceedings in the Commons were broadcast live by radio in a month-long experiment, but television cameras were again barred, by 12 votes.

Timothy West was crowned **Edward the Seventh** in a series that won critical acclaim, topped the ratings and was voted Best Drama Series of 1975 by the British Academy of Film and Television Arts. (ATV)

Celebrity Squares, an Anglicised version of a top American quiz show in which contestants decided whether guest celebrities had answered questions correctly. (ATV)

My Brother's Keeper took a humorous look at the controversial subject of law and order, with George Layton as a policeman, Jonathan Lynn as his wastrel twin. (Granada)

Joy Adamson's story of how she reared the lioness Elsa – subject of two British films – was the basis for **Born Free,** an American series filmed in Kenya.

Adapted from A. J. Cronin's best-selling novel of the Thirties, **The Stars Look Down** was the story of a north eastern mining community during the early years of this century. (Granada)

The Sweeney, a filmed crime series, set new standards for realistic fights, dramatic car chases and crackling dialogue. John Thaw starred as Det.-Insp. Jack Regan. (Thames)

Nutritionist Dr. Magnus Pyke (65), became an unlikely TV star as a resident expert in the popular science show, **Don't Ask Me,** which was regularly in the Top Twenty. (Yorkshire)

A bold documentary venture, **The Naked Civil Servant** was the dramatised story of the flamboyant homosexual Quentin Crisp, played by John Hurt. The role won him a B.A.F.T.A. award as best actor of the year. (Thames)

Hollywood's Ann-Margret sang and danced in a lavish musical, **Ann-Margret Olsson,** one of ITV's shows with a ready market in other countries (ATV)

Akenfield, Peter Hall's sensitive film about a Suffolk village, made history by being shown simultaneously in the cinema and on ITV. It was part-financed by London Weekend.

Gerry and Sylvia Anderson employed their special effects experience, gained on puppet series such as **Thunderbirds,** to produce **Space 1999,** a lunar epic. (ATV)

1975

Carry On Laughing,
television version of
the cinema's
bold, box-office
romps. (ATV)

A thriller serial – a
comparative rarity
among TV series –
The Hanged Man
starred Colin Blakely
as a tough
construction company
boss. (Yorkshire)

A Place In Europe
showed famous
houses and palaces
where families still
live – including
Vaux-le-Vicomte
in France. (Thames)

Jane Austen and Her World, a tribute to the author of Emma on the 200th anniversary of her birth. (Southern)

Derek Farr starred in Nightingale's Boys, a seven-part story about an elderly teacher who set out to discover what had become of the pupils from his class of 1949. (Granada)

The boom in nostalgia inspired Get Some In, a comedy series about RAF National Servicemen in the Fifties, with Tony Selby as a corporal. (Thames)

215

Graham Greene allowed his work to be televised for the first time in **Shades of Greene.** Donald Pleasence, John Le Mesurier and Bill Fraser starred in this one, **The Root of All Evil.** (Thames)

Comedian-turned-actor Bill Maynard played a widower with a roving eye in the comedy series, **The Life of Riley.** (Granada)

As comedies became more realistic, Rosemary Leach and Bernard Hepton starred as a couple frustrated by dull routine in a new domestic series, **Sadie, It's Cold Outside.** (Thames)

The documentary **Johnny Go Home** created nationwide concern with its relation of what can happen to youngsters attracted by the lights of London. It was adjudged Best Factual Programme of 1975 by B.A.F.T.A. (Yorkshire)

Dr. No, first of six James Bond (Sean Connery) films acquired by ITV, caused a new wave of 007 fever with its small-screen showing. Discussions began about the need for extra time on television for interpreting the news and setting it in a wider context.

National Theatre Director Peter Hall became presenter of the arts magazine **Aquarius.**

In a year designated as International Women's Year, when a woman became IBA chairman, Margery Baker wrote and produced **A Place In Europe;** Andrea Wonfor produced **The First Train Now Arriving,** a documentary on the birth of railways; Jean Marsh was named the Variety Club's ITV personality for her part in creating, and performance in, **Upstairs, Downstairs;** ITN's Diana Edwards-Jones received an award for her direction of the 1974 General Election programmes, and the first products of Verity Lambert's 1974 appointment as Thames Television's Controller of Drama reached the screen.

217

1976

ITV approached its 21st Anniversary with a wider range than ever before, offering more news, current affairs, documentary, arts, religious and educational programmes. And it was still the most popular channel with the majority of viewers.

But the year was overshadowed by the uncertainty of "waiting for Annan"–the report of Lord Annan's Committee on the Future of Broadcasting.

Meanwhile, Harold Wilson handed over the Premiership to James Callaghan; Concorde entered regular service; and the sale of colour TV sets, which had slumped after the imposition of a 25 per cent VAT rate in 1975, was given new encouragement when Chancellor Denis Healey slashed the rate by half.

Luke's Kingdom was an "Australian Western" series about British settlers in New South Wales during the days of covered wagons.

1976

The International **Pop Proms** were devised by John Hamp, Head of Light Entertainment, to do for pop music what the Albert Hall Proms have done for the Classics. A 50-strong orchestra in the King's Hall, Manchester, backed international stars before an audience of 4,000. (Granada)

Life among the "never had it so good" working class was the theme of the comedy series **Yus My Dear**, with Arthur Mullard as a council house-dwelling bricklayer, Queenie Watts as his demanding wife. (LWT)

New star Marti Caine, a zany comedienne discovered on the **New Faces** talent show, won her own series, **Another Drop of Marti Caine.** (ATV)

Jack Parnell and his Orchestra have provided the backing music for many of ITV's spectacular shows. But with the current nostalgia for the sounds of the Forties, they took the limelight in **The Jack Parnell Big Band Show.** (ATV)

Hughie Green, who has presented talent shows on ITV since 1956, proved his own versatility by impersonating eight characters in **Hughie's Full House.** Here he joins the minstrels. (Thames)

221

Clayhanger was a 26-part serial based on Arnold Bennett's trilogy of novels about family life in the Staffordshire Potteries during the latter part of the 19th century. Peter McEnery and Janet Suzman headed the cast of over 100. (ATV)

Destination America, a documentary in eight parts, told the story of Europeans who have emigrated to the New World in the past 150 years and helped to shape its character and destiny. (Thames)

1976

The Fortune Hunters, adapted from a West End of London stage production, starred Robert Morley as a judge who had to decide on a disputed will. (Anglia)

Rock Follies, whose style was adapted from the Hollywood musicals of the Thirties, followed three girl rock singers in their determined bid for stardom. (Thames)

The Fosters was the first British situation comedy in which all the main characters were black. The series looked at the way a West Indian family coped with the pressures of life in London. (LWT)

Red Letter Day took turning points in its subjects' lives as a common theme. In Jack Rosenthal's **Ready when you are, Mr. McGill,** a film extra was given his first speaking role. (Granada)

Richard Carpenter, creator of **Catweazle**, continued to place figures from the past in modern contexts with **The Ghosts of Motley Hall**, a series for children in which five historical spectres haunted a house together. (Granada)

The Feathered Serpent was an adventure series for children set in the Mexico of the Toltecs in 750 A.D. (Thames)

Following their successful series on BBC Radio, John Junkin, Tim Brooke-Taylor and Barry Cryer transferred the quickfire comedy show, **Hello Cheeky,** to television. (Yorkshire)

A lavish production of J. M. Barrie's **Peter Pan** starred the elfin Mia Farrow as Peter and Danny Kaye as a lively Captain Hook. (ATV)

1976

Andrea Newman adapted her novel, **Bouquet of Barbed Wire,** for a TV series. It was the story of a man's obsessive love for his daughter – with Frank Finlay and Susan Penhaligon in the main roles – and audiences called for a sequel. (LWT)

The murder of Kenneth Lennon, who tipped-off the Special Branch about IRA activities in England, was reconstructed in the documentary, **Death of an Informer.** (ATV)

A team of clim[...] turned camerame[...] **Matterhor[...]** first filmed re[...] of an attem[...] the North Face. ([...]

Brian Young, Director General of the IBA since 1970, was knighted, and Sir Lew Grade received a life peerage.

ITV mourned the death of two of its most popular stars – Angela Baddeley, who played Mrs. Bridges in **Upstairs, Downstairs,** and Sidney James, of **Bless This House.**

Pat Phoenix, the popular Elsie Tanner in **Coronation Street,** returned to the serial after three years on the stage.

Alastair Burnet, for many years ITV's front man for big occasions, resigned the editorship of the Daily Express – a position he had held since 1974 – and returned to the ITN team.

Joanna Lumley was chosen to be Patrick Macnee's co-star in a new series of **The Avengers.**

The Prince of Wales introduced **Prince Charles and Canterbury Cathedral** to aid an appeal for restoration funds.

Hughie Green presented his 400th. **Opportunity Knocks!**

Those Wonderful TV Times was a quiz show about programmes and players in the 21 years of ITV.

1977

The long-awaited Annan Report was published in March. It had praise for ITV programmes which it held to be generally the equal of the BBC's, while in the presentation of news ITV surpassed the BBC. However, the Report recommended that a fourth TV channel should be controlled by a new Open Broadcasting Authority. While awaiting a White Paper setting out the Government's intentions, the ITV companies continued to press for the fourth channel to be ITV2.

Meanwhile, television licences were increased to £21 for colour and £9 for black and white.

It was the Queen's Jubilee Year, marking the 25th anniversary of her accession, and Prince Charles made his TV debut on all channels to launch a Jubilee Appeal for money to help young people help others. ITV lost coverage of celebrations in London because of a pay dispute involving production assistants at Thames. Firemen throughout the country went on strike and there was also a dispute at the Grunwick film processing laboratories in London notable for massive picketing. But the Laker Skytrain got airborne to America, where Jimmy Carter became President and went on television to warn of the need for fuel economies.

Portraying Christ on screen is always a challenge, but Christians and unbelievers alike acclaimed Robert Powell's mesmeric performance in **Jesus of Nazareth,** a six-part co-production with Italian TV which Franco Zeffirelli directed with a cast of international stars in North Africa. (ATV)

Another six-part Biblical co-production with Italian TV was **Moses – The Lawgiver,** filmed in the Holy Land with Burt Lancaster playing the title role and his first-ever TV part. (ATV)

The Professionals established new action heroes in Doyle and Brodie (Martin Shaw and Lewis Collins), fast-shooting agents of CI5, an anti-terrorist unit commanded by Cowley (Gordon Jackson). (LWT)

Lord Olivier confessed; "I have stood out stiffly and coldly and pompously about TV for too long"; in **Laurence Olivier Presents** he produced and starred in "the best plays" of various years, including 1973's **Saturday, Sunday, Monday** by Eduardo de Filippo, about an Italian family dinner. (Granada)

Life in a London lodging house in the early days of World War Two was recreated in **London Belongs to Me,** a serialisation of the best-seller by Norman Collins, though the action ranged as far as the beaches of Dunkirk. (Thames)

Concern with opportunities for women was reflected by **The Foundation** in which Davina Price (played by Lynette Davies) took her late husband's place in a company boardroom. (ATV)

One of the most popular single plays of the year was **The Dame of Sark**, set during the German occupation of the Channel Isles, with Celia Johnson in the title role. (Anglia)

Any subject was suitable for situation comedy series by now . . . even an unmarried mother. Paula Wilcox starred as one in **Miss Jones and Son.** (Thames)

Love for Lydia, a 13-part adaptation from a novel by H.E. Bates, was shot largely on location with mobile video equipment and a new star in Mel Martin. (LWT)

Wedding of the year was that of abrasive Len Fairclough and his shop manageress, Rita Littlewood, in **Coronation Street.** (Granada)

Robin's Nest, with Richard O'Sullivan, followed **George and Mildred** as another spin-off from the earlier comedy series, **Man About the House.** (Thames)

The world of E.W. Hornung's Edwardian cricketer-cracksman, **Raffles,** was lovingly evoked in a series in which the gentleman of crime was smoothly played by Anthony Valentine. (Yorkshire)

Ian Curteis pioneered the writing of "faction", using real persons and events as material for drama; his **Philby, Burgess and Maclean** had look-alikes playing the traitors who fled to Russia. (Granada)

237

Hard Times, a serialisation of the moving novel by Charles Dickens, was a triumph and took the top TV award in the New York International Film Festival. (Granada)

In the business jungle Arthur Prufrock Devenish was a tiger . . . with rubber teeth. Dinsdale Landen played **Devenish,** an incompetent games company executive in this sit-com. (Granada)

An extra Y chromosome [in] the body makes one tall [and] likely to be a criminal, according to a [con]troversial theory. **The [YY Man** exploited this [th]eory in a thriller series [abou]t Spider Scott, a lanky [c]at burglar used by the [g]overnment. (Granada)

[Ri]chmal Crompton's **Just William** stories were [f]aithfully re-told in their [ori]ginal 1928 setting, with [a] 14-year-old Adrian Dannatt as the [tro]uble-prone lad. (LWT)

Brian Walden gave up his seat as a Labour MP to become presenter of **Weekend World,** succeeding Peter Jay. Experimental breakfast-time transmissions took place in Yorkshire and the North East between 8.30 and 9.30am. IBA research into digital equipment reached a point where its engineers were able to demonstrate all the major component parts of an all-digital TV studio of the future. **Alternative 3** was a play disguised as a documentary which had scientists disappearing from the face of the Earth because of pollution to colonise Mars; given realism by the use of newsreel film of disasters, and the presence of ex-newscaster Tim Brinton, it fooled and frightened many viewers in a manner reminiscent of Orson Welles' **War of the Worlds** on American Radio. Bamber Gascoigne visited 30 countries to write and narrate **The Christians,** a 13-part documentary series about the importance and influence of Christianity over the years. Much-travelled film-maker Antony Thomas caused a storm – of complaint and praise – with **The South African Experience,** a four-part series in which he reported on the life and conditions of black workers. **The Krypton Factor,** a quiz games series, tested brains and brawn through a contest of physical endurance and mental agility.

1978

The Government White Paper on broadcasting supported the Annan recommendation of a fourth channel controlled by an Open Broadcasting Authority and financed partly by government money and partly by advertising. The Conservatives pledged themselves to a channel controlled by the IBA and financed by advertising at no cost to the taxpayer. TV licence fees rose again – to £25 for colour and £10 for black and white – to aid the BBC which was in financial difficulties. London Weekend Television reached an agreement with the Football League giving ITV exclusive rights to televise League games for three years; however, after fierce protests from the BBC it was eventually agreed that the two networks should continue to share fixtures. In the World Cup in Argentina Scotland's football team was humiliated; England's did not even get there.

Publication of The Times and Sunday Times was suspended while the management sought to sign deals with unions.

Edward and Mrs. Simpson told the story of Edward VIII's love for an American divorcee which resulted in his abdication and exile. BAFTA acclaimed it best drama series of the year and Edward Fox best actor for his portrayal of the King. (Thames)

Lillie Langtry had featured briefly in **Edward the Seventh** as his favourite companion when Prince of Wales; in **Lillie** she was the subject of a series which won Francesca Annis, who played her, the BAFTA award as best actress. (LWT)

Geraldine McEwan played a Scottish schoolteacher with radical ideas (for the 1930s) in **The Prime of Miss Jean Brodie**, a series based on the novel by Muriel Spark. (STV)

Betzi was a single play about Napoleon's attachment to a young girl during his last months of exile on St. Helena. Frank Finlay played the deposed emperor and Lucy Gutteridge the girl. (Anglia)

Melvyn Bragg and Ken Russell made **Clouds of Glory** about the Lakeland poets, Coleridge and Wordsworth. The programmes won a premier gold award at the New York International Film Festival. (Granada)

A new and original funny man is a rarity. ITV gambled by making six hour-long programmes titled **An Audience With Jasper Carrott** but the Birmingham comic (formerly Bob Davis) won a Pye Award as "Outstanding New Personality". (LWT)

In the most publicised cross-channel switch of the year, **Morecambe and Wise,** firmly established as Britain's best-loved comics, returned to ITV where they had made their names. (Thames)

In **Warrior Queen** Sian Phillips starred as Queen Boudicca, who led the British in a revolt against the Romans in 59AD. (Thames)

By Alan Bennett . . . **Six Plays** showcased the writer's inventive but peculiar sense of humour. **The Old Crowd,** in particular, delighted but perplexed critics. (LWT)

Richard O'Sullivan switched from situation comedy to a swashbuckling role as the highwayman, **Dick Turpin.** (LWT)

Spearhead had soldiers as its heroes as a change from policemen. It concerned the adventures of men of an army unit held in readiness to go anywhere. (Southern)

The Muppet Show was now established as a cult; many internationally-famous stars appeared with the puppets. (ATV)

Loved by young people, possibly loathed by older ones, **The Kenny Everett Video Show,** a mad mixture of music, dancing and cartoon, exploited TV technology to the full, and won a British Academy award for light entertainment. (Thames)

A pioneer stripper was the subject of the dramatised documentary, **The One and Only Phyllis Dixey,** with Lesley-Anne Down as the so-demure teaser. (Thames)

The Saint, the debonair hero of the Leslie Charteris stories, formerly played on ITV by Roger Moore, made a comeback played by Ian Ogilvy in **Return of the Saint.** (ATV)

Another new quiz show – developed from a Spanish one – was **3-2-1** in which couples could win £1,000 or a dustbin. Ted Rogers compered with the aid of no fewer than six hostesses, the Gentle Secs. (Yorkshire)

249

A new private eye hero was Cockney James **Hazell,** creation of Terry Venables and Gordon Williams, played by Nicholas Ball. (Thames)

Anna Ford joined **News at Ten** as a newscaster; male viewers fell in love with her on sight and the Radio Industries' Club made her "Newscaster of the Year". (ITN)

Reporter Michael Nicholson and an ITN film crew were missing in Angola for 110 days during which time they had to march 1,500 miles with rebel forces evading government troops. After a daring rescue, Nicholson's report won him the Royal Television Society's first TV Reporter of the Year award. (ITN)

Not all the Ge were villains and the British were h in **Enemy at the D** drama series set Channel Isles c World War Two. Germany was a countries which sh it. (

John Mortimer QC the BAFTA w. award for his invent hack barrister Ho Rumpole, played b McKern in **Rump** **the Bailey.** (Tha

Streets which had built behind stud Elstree to represen Potteries in **Clayha** were converted Elizabethan Londo **Will Shakespea** roistering series Tim Curry as the (

IBA engineers developed a mobile earth station for use in experimental satellite transmissions. In its first public demonstration, television pictures were sent from the Wembley Conference Centre by way of a European Orbital Test Satellite launched earlier in the year and included live in a news bulletin; this won ITN the Royal Television Society's International Current Affairs Award for new techniques. **This Week** was given a new title, **TV Eye,** and its first programme was on the birth to an Oldham woman of the first "test tube baby", conceived by fertilisation outside the mother's body. Bearded botanist David Bellamy told the story of the evolution of life on earth in **Botanic Man** which won BAFTA's Richard Dimbleby Award for the year's most important personal contribution to factual TV. **The South Bank Show,** edited and presented by Melvyn Bragg, succeeded **Aquarius** as ITV's main arts programme. **Mayerling,** a special programme, which followed Kenneth MacMillan's ballet from conception to production, won the music category of the prestigious Prix Italia. From the same studio as **The Sweeney** came **Out,** another tough thriller starring Tom Bell as Frank Ross, back in his London haunts after an eight-year prison sentence for bank robbery and determined to discover who "grassed".

1979

The future of the fourth channel was finally decided by a general election. The Conservatives won, Margaret Thatcher became Britain's first woman Prime Minister and her government swiftly announced that the channel would be introduced under the control of the IBA.

With the future clear at last, the IBA began public meetings to canvass opinions from the viewers before advertising franchises for a new ITV era to start in 1982. But it was ITV's blackest year. Except in the Channel Isles its screens were blank for 11 weeks in the autumn because of a technicians' strike. This was mainly about pay but also concerned the introduction of new technology, particularly Electronic News Gathering, involving the use of lightweight TV cameras in place of film cameras. During the year ITN was permitted to use ENG for a six months trial but the unions jibbed at permanent national agreements.

Licence fees went up again – to £34 for colour and £12 for monochrome. Rioting in Iran and the exit of the Shah was followed by the return from exile of the Ayatollah Khomeini who proclaimed the country an Islamic republic. The plight of the Vietnamese boat people – refugees who fled from the Communists – caused world-wide concern. Earl Mountbatten of Burma was killed by a terrorist bomb on his boat while on holiday with his family in Ireland.

The life of an army bomb disposal officer during the blitz on London was the subject of the drama series, **Danger UXB**.
(Thames)

1979

Another costume drama series, **Flambards,** based on books by Kathleen Peyton, concerned an orphan girl in Edwardian times, brought up in a decaying house by a crippled, hard-drinking uncle with two eligible sons. (Yorkshire)

Kidnapped, a serialisation of R.L. Stevenson's Scottish story, had a cast including German and French artists; it was a co-production with German Television. (HTV)

rticulate layabout,
off the state while
uncing the system,
he unconventional
of the situation
edy, **Shelley.** He was
ed by Hywel
ett. (Thames)

A spin-off from **Budgie** in 1971, **Charles Endell Esq** began with the return from prison to his native Glasgow of the Soho entrepreneur played by Iain Cuthbertson. (STV)

1979

Nostalgia for the rock'n'rolling Fifties and Sixties was catered for by a revival of **Oh Boy!** with such durable stars as Joe Brown. (ATV)

The importance of casting was demonstrated by **Minder;** the chemistry between Dennis Waterman as a bodyguard for hire, and George Cole as his shifty manager, made them a popular team. (Thames)

In the documentary, **Kitty – Return to Auschwitz,** Polish-born Kitty Hart travelled from Birmingham with her son to show him the concentration camp in which, as a teenager during World War Two, she saw thousands murdered. (Yorkshire)

e **Mallens,** based on a novel by Catherine ookson and set in 19th century Northumberland, llowed the fortunes of impoverished Squire homas Mallen and his eirs, distinguished on male side by a streak white hair. (Granada)

Quatermass brought back to TV one of science fiction's great characters, created by Nigel Kneale 27 years earlier; the professor, played by Sir John Mills, was seen fighting to save the world from anarchy. (Thames)

A magazine's advice columnist who could help readers with their problems but was unable to solve her own, was the heroine of a comedy series, **Agony.** (LWT)

Tropic was a serial based on the bawdy best-seller by Leslie Thomas about sex on a suburban housing estate. (ATV)

Another spin-off, this time from **Upstairs, Downstairs,** was **Thomas and Sarah,** which followed the later escapades of its wily Welsh chauffeur and pert parlourmaid, played by John Alderton and Pauline Collins. (LWT)

A former jockey turned private investigator, who tackled racing swindles, was the hero of **The Racing Game,** a thriller series by ex-jockey Dick Francis. (Yorkshire)

Dick Barton, the pioneering secret agent and former star of radio, came to television with his aides, Snowey and Jock. (Southern)

After Julius, a trilogy by Elizabeth Jane Howard, told of love in a country house during the course of a weekend in 1960 and was appropriately shown on a Friday, Saturday and Sunday. (Yorkshire)

Tales of the Unexpected were adaptations of twist-in-the-tail stories by Roald Dahl; **Neck** starred Joan Collins as a titled lady and Sir John Gielgud as her butler, Jelks. (Anglia)

The Sound of the Guns, about newspapermen in Cyprus during the Suez crisis of 1956, was a first play for television by journalist James Cameron who was there at the time. (Granada)

261

The Jimmy Edwards comedy family, **The Glums,** originally on radio in the Fifties and revived as a segment of **Bruce's Big Night,** became a series in its own right. (LWT)

Joanna Lumley and David McCallum played supernatural troubleshooters, aliens with extrasensory powers, in the twice-weekly **Sapphire and Steel.** (ATV)

Ivor Novello's 40-year-old romantic musical, **The Dancing Years,** set in Vienna between the World Wars, was revived with Anthony Valentine in the leading role. (ATV)

The walking, tal scarecrow of Bar. Euphan Todd's **Wo Gummidge** sto formerly a radio se was brought to life new generatic children by Jon Pertw (South

The IBA's transportable space terminal was used for the first satellite transmissions from Eire during the Pope's visit. In West Yorkshire the IBA opened its 500th transmitter. Oracle, the ITV teletext service, expanded into a seven-days-a-week service. Viewers sent in more than £7 million after **Year Zero – The Silent Death of Cambodia** in which campaigning journalist John Pilger revealed the plight of Kampuchea since the Vietnamese routed the Khmer Rouge; the Broadcasting Press Guild voted it "best documentary of the year." **Rampton: The Secret Hospital** caused questions in Parliament and police inquiries and won the Royal Television Society's award for investigative journalism. Director John Willis interviewed more than 150 former staff, ex-patients and relatives and itemised 800 allegations of brutality. To mark the International Year of the Child, the European Broadcasting Union commissioned the **Survival** team to make a film to be shown simultaneously in all 31 member countries; **The Seas Must Live** was intended to alert young people to the crisis facing the oceans of the world. Gus Macdonald introduced **Camera,** a 13-part series on early photography. BAFTA's Shell Award for the most effective contribution to the understanding of trade and industry was awarded to Granada's **Nuts and Bolts of the Economy.**

1980

In its silver jubilee year ITV began a new period of expansion and progress. The IBA advertised new franchises to begin in January 1982, the geographical areas remaining unchanged except that the Midlands and Southern England were to become two-centre regions like HTV, with its studios in Bristol and Cardiff. The IBA also floated the possibility of a national licence for breakfast-time television based around news and current affairs.

The fourth channel was scheduled to begin in all regions except the Channel Isles by November 1982. Meanwhile the BBC was compelled to begin a programme of cut backs and economies.

Athletes were pressed to boycott the Olympic Games in Moscow as a protest at the Soviet invasion of Afghanistan. New elections in Rhodesia resulted in Robert Mugabe becoming Prime Minister and an official change of the country's name to Zimbabwe.

New technology made it possible for **Hollywood,** the story of the silent movies, to screen excerpts from historic films as the makers had intended them to be seen. (Thames)

1980

For the first time, television was allowed to dramatise an Agatha Christie mystery; it was **Why Didn't They Ask Evans?** with an aristocratic, high-spirited sleuth, Lady Frances Derwent. (LWT)

In **The Further Adventures of Oliver Twist,** David Butler carried on the story of Oliver and the Artful Dodger from the point where Charles Dickens' novel ended. (ATV)

In **The Faith Brown Chat Show** the star impersonated many women celebrities including Margaret Thatcher as Wonder Woman. (LWT)

Film cameras visited 80 locations for **The English Garden,** a history narrated by Sir John Gielgud. (Thames)

The portrayal of police on TV came full circle; they were upright and honest again in **The Gentle Touch,** a serial about a beautiful woman Detective Inspector, widowed when her PC husband was shot. (LWT)

Bruce Forsyth bounced back after some criticism with a new quiz show, **Play Your Cards Right.** (LWT)

The problems of retirement were the subject of Vince Powell's comedy series, **Young at Heart,** in which Sir John Mills played a pottery worker compulsorily scrapped at 65. (ATV)

1980

Millions watched the live coverage of the dramatic ending to the May siege of the Iranian Embassy in London. (ITN)

A diplomatic row was caused by Antony Thomas's dramatised documentary **Death of a Princess,** in which he unravelled the story of a Saudi Arabian princess publicly executed for adultery in 1977. (ATV)

The Nesbitts are Coming
was an unusual comedy
series about a family of
petty crooks fighting
with the law as they
wandered from town to
town – singing.
(Yorkshire)

Expert knowledge was
no longer essential for
quiz shows; in new ones
like Bob Monkhouse's
Family Fortunes families
could win a jackpot of
£1,000 by guessing
answers given earlier by
a panel. (ATV)

her, more realistic
na for children was
rovided by **Noah's
Castle** set in a near
future when
hyper-inflation had
resulted in food
ortages, leading to
g, fighting and near
narchy. (Southern)

A new serial, **For
Maddie with Love,**
starred Ian Hendry and
Nyree Dawn Porter as a
happy couple whose
marriage was suddenly
threatened. (ATV)

A different kind of police hero was Sgt. **Cribb**, a Victorian detective from the novels of Peter Lovesey, played by Alan Dobie. (Granada)

In **The Spoils of War**, John Finch, who scripted **A Family at War**, examined the effects of World War Two on two families in the Lake District between 1945 and 1952. (Granada)

Fox was the story hardy South Lor family with P Vaughan as its p head. Staunch fa loyalty was set agai backgrour underworld acti (Thar

Following an agreement between ITV and the BBC over coverage of League football, ITV switched its coverage of Saturday matches from Sunday afternoons to Saturday evenings – a pattern to alternate yearly with the BBC. ITV acquired the rights to show the **Miss United Kingdom** contest and its sequel, **Miss World.** The ENG revolution gathered speed; Grampian TV followed Channel in switching news coverage entirely from film to electronic cameras. Jonathan Dimbleby began a series of documentary programmes. Lorraine Chase, who made her name as a Cockney in Campari commercials, starred in her own series, **The Other 'Arf. Coronation Street** celebrated its 2,000th episode. Meanwhile, in **Crossroads,** David Hunter, co-owner of the motel, married Barbara Brady, but the serial was cut back from four days weekly to three by the IBA to improve the quality.

Further details of actors and characters pictured throughout this book.

Foreword
The Marriage of Figaro: Marius Rinsler (Dr. Bartolo), Knut Skran (Figaro), Benjamin Luxon (Count Almaviva), Bernard Dickerson (Don Curzio), Nucci Condo (Marcellina). **Upstairs, Downstairs:** Simon Williams (James Bellamy), Lesley-Anne Down (Georgina Worsley). **How The West Was Won:** James Arness (Zeb MacAhan), Eva Marie Saint (Kate MacAhan).

1955
8/9 **ITV's Inaugural Dinner:** Postmaster General, Dr. Charles Hill; Lord Mayor of London, Sir Seymour Howard; Chairman of ITA, Sir Kenneth Clark.
10/11 **The Scarlet Pimpernel:** Patrick Troughton (Sir Andrew Ffoulkes), Marius Goring (Sir Percy Blakeney), Anthony Newlands (Lord Richard Hastings). **The Adventures of Robin Hood:** Richard Greene (Robin Hood), Patricia Driscoll (Marian), Alexander Gauge (Friar Tuck).
12/13 **Colonel March of Scotland Yard:** Ewan Roberts (Ames), Boris Karloff (Colonel March). **The Importance of Being Earnest:** Margaret Leighton (Gwendoline), John Gielgud (Ernest), Dame Edith Evans (Lady Bracknell).
14/15 **Take Your Pick:** Alec Dane, Bob Danvers-Walker, Michael Miles.
16/17 **Douglas Fairbanks Presents – Success Train:** Douglas Fairbanks (Mark Terry).

1956
20/21 **The 64,000 Question:** Supt. Fabian of Scotland Yard, Jerry Desmonde. **Sir Lancelot:** Zena Walker William Russell.
22/23 **The Count of Monte Cristo:** Robert Cawdron (Rico), George Dolenz (Count of Monte Cristo), Nick Cravat (Jacopo). **Armchair Theatre – The Outsider:** David Kossoff (Ragatzy), Adrienne Corri (Lalange).
24/25 **Son of Fred:** Spike Milligan, Peter Sellers, Kenneth Connor, Graham Stark, Richard Lester. **The Buccaneers:** Robert Shaw, Thomas G. Duggan.
26/27 **The Arthur Haynes Show:** Dermot Kelly, Arthur Haynes.

1957
30/31 **No Hiding Place:** Eric Lander (Sgt. Harry Baxter), Raymond Francis (Det.-Insp. Tom Lockhart).
32/33 **Lunch Box:** Alan Grahame, Lionel Rubin, Ken Ingerfield, Jerry Allen, Noele Gordon. **Mark Saber:** Neil McCallum, Donald Gray, Honor Blackman, John McLaren.
34/35 **Yes, It's the Cathode-Ray Tube Show:** Michael Bentine, David Nettheim, Peter Sellers.
36/37 **Jim's Inn:** Jimmy Hanley, Maggie Hanley. **The Army Game:** Geoffrey Sumner (Major "Piggy" Upshot-Bagley), Norman Rossington (Pte. "CupCake" Cook), Bernard Bresslaw (Pte. "Popeye" Popplewell), Charles Hawtrey (Pte. "Professor" Hatchet), William Hartnell (CSM Bullimore).

1958
38/39 **The Larkins:** Ruth Trouncer (Joyce Larkin), Barbara Mitchell (Hetty Prout), David Kossoff (Alf Larkin), Peggy Mount (Ada Larkin), Ronan O'Casey (Jeff Rogers), Shaun O'Riordan (Eddie Rogers).
40/41 **The Sunday Break:** John Gilbert with club members.
44/45 **Educating Archie:** Dick Emery, Freddie Sales, Archie Andrews, Peter Brough, Ray Barrett.

1959
48/49 **Holiday Town Parade:** Drum Majorette Eira Roberts, Jill Laurence.
50/51 **Probation Officer:** David Davies (Jim Blake), John Paul (Philip Main). **Knight Errant:** John Turner (Adam Knight), Kay Callard (Liz Parrish).
52/53 **Four Just Men:** Vittorio de Sica (Ricco Roccari), Jack Hawkins (Ben Manfred, MP), Dan Dailey (Tim Collier), Richard Conte (Jeff Ryder).
54/55 **Skyport:** French Customs official, George Moon (Ginger Smart). **Armchair Theatre – No Tram to Lime Street:** Jack Hedley (Billy Mack), Billie Whitelaw (Betty).

1960
58/59 **Danger Man:** Patrick McGoohan (John Drake). **Deadline Midnight:** Mary Law, Peter Frazer, Armine Sandford. Foreground: Jeremy Young, Glyn Houston.
60/61 **Police Surgeon:** Ian Hendry, Olive McFarland, John Warwick. **Our House:** Norman Rossington (Gordon Brent), Joan Sims (Daisy Burke), Ina de la Hayes (Mrs. Iliffe), Frank Pettingell (Capt. Iliffe), Frederick Peisley (Herbert Keane), Leigh Madison (Marcia Hatton), Trader Faulkner (Stephen Hatton). Foreground: Hattie Jacques (Georgina Ruddy), Charles Hawtrey (Simon Willow).
62/63 **The Royal Variety Performance:** The Crazy Gang – Charlie Naughton, Jimmy Gold, "Monsewer" Eddie Gray, Bud Flanagan, Teddy Knox, Jimmy Nervo.
66/67 **Mess Mates:** Fulton Mackay (Willie McGinnis), Sam Kydd (Croaker Jones), Archie Duncan (Capt. Biskett), Victor Maddern (The Mate), Dermot Kelly (Blarney Finnigan). **Kipps:** Sheila Steafel (Flo Bates), Brian Murray (Kipps).

1961
70/71 **Harpers West C** Jane Muir (Frances Peters), Jan Holden (Harriet Carr). **Family Solicitor:** Edwin Apps Tony Wright, Josephi Price.
74/75 **Armchair Theat The Rose Affair:** Josep O'Conor (Dr. O'Riord Harold Lang (Johnson butler), Anthony Quay (Betumain).

1962
80/81 **Electra:** Aspassi Papathanassiou (Elect Anthi Kariofili (Chrysothemis). **Man o the World:** Craig Stev Tracy Reed.
84/85 **Armchair Theatr Afternoon of a Nymph** Janet Munro (Elaine), Ian Hendry (David Simpson). **Bulldog Bre** Donald Churchill, Ama Barrie.
86/87 **Saki:** Marc Burns Fenella Fielding.

1963
88/89 **The Plane Maker** Patrick Wymark (John Wilder), Jack Watling (Don Henderson).
90/91 **The Human Jungl** Herbert Lom (Dr. Roge Corder). **Our Man at St. Marks:** Leslie Phillips (Rev. Andrew Parker).
92/93 **The Victorians –** **Waters Run Deep:** Joy Heron (Mrs. Sternhold Ingrid Hafner (Emily Mildmay), Michael Barrington (Mr. Potter) Barrie Ingham (Capt. Hawksley).
94/95 **Crane:** Sam Kyd (Orlando), Patrick Alle (Crane).

9 Crossroads : Noele
don (Meg Richardson).
101 A Midsummer
t's Dream : Peter
garde (Oberon),
a Massey (Titania).
103 Fire Crackers :
d Marks (Charlie),
Baker (Jumbo),
ew Robinson
rpin), Sydney Bromley
rie Willie), Ronnie
ie (Loverboy).
105 A Choice of
ard – Blithe Spirit :
na Dunham (Elvira),
ie Jacques (Madame
ti), Griffith Jones
rles). A Little Big
ness : Billy Russell
rlie), Francis
hews (Simon), David
off (Marcus
erman), Martin
r (Lazlo). The Other
: Michael Caine
rge Grant).
107 The Sullavan
hers : David Sumner
rick Sullavan), Mary
ton (Beth Sullavan),
iel Evans (John
avan), Hugh Manning
ert Sullavan),
hony Bate (Paul
avan).

5
111 Redcap : John
w (Sgt. John Mann).
t Page Story : Roddy
illan (Alec Ritchie),
k Godfrey (Danny
ant), John Bennett
Boscombe). The Man
om 17 : Michael
ridge (Lt. Dimmock),
ard Vernon
enshaw).
113 The Successor :
mas Baptiste
rdinal of Uganda),
ert Davies (Cardinal
ologna), Tony
dman (Cardinal
aris), Robert Lee
rdinal of Macao).
eground : John Welsh
rdinal of Milan), Peter
ley (Cardinal Ricci).
od and Thunder –
men Beware Women :
ford Evans (The Duke),
na Rigg (Bianca).
/115 Riviera Police :
offrey Frederick (Supt.
am Hunter), Brian Spink
sp. Legrand). Court
rtial : Peter Graves
ajor Frank Whittaker),
dford Dillman (Capt.
vid Young).
/117 Blackmail – First
ender : Ann Bell (Edna),
dley Foster (Joey
iffin).

1966
120/121 Intrigue :
Caroline Mortimer (Val
Spencer), Edward Judd
(Gavin Grant). Weavers
Green : Grant Taylor (Alan
Armstrong), Eric Flynn
(Geoffrey Toms), Megs
Jenkins (Dotty Armstrong),
Richard Coleman (Jack
Royston). The Baron :
Steve Forrest (John
Mannering), Nosher
Powell (Charlie).
122/123 Mystery and
Imagination – The
Phantom Lover : Virginia
McKenna (Alice Oke),
David Buck (Richard
Beckett). The Informer : Ian
Hendry (Alex Lambert),
Heather Sears (Janet
Lambert), Jean Marsh
(Sylvia).
124/125 Orlando : David
Munro (Steve), Judy
Robinson (Jenny), Sam
Kydd (Orlando). George
and the Dragon : Keith
Marsh (Ralph), Peggy
Mount (Gabrielle), Sidney
James (George). All
Square : Michael Bentine,
Deryck Guyler, Leon Thau,
Benny Lee.
126/127 The Stories of D. H.
Lawrence – Strike Pay :
Angela Morant (Mrs.
Radford), John Ronane
(Tom Radford). Nelson –
A Study in Miniature :
Michael Bryant (Nelson),
Rachel Roberts (Lady
Hamilton). World Cup :
Martin Peters, Roger Hunt,
Geoff Hurst, Bobby Moore,
Ray Wilson, George
Cohen, Bobby Charlton.

1967
128/129 News at Ten :
Reginald Bosanquet,
Andrew Gardner.
130/131 The Golden Shot :
Anita Richardson, Andrea
Lloyd, Bob Monkhouse,
Carol Dilworth.
Inheritance : Thelma
Whiteley (Mary
Bamforth), John Thaw (Will
Oldroyd).
132/133 No, That's Me
Over Here : Ivor Dean,
Ronnie Corbett. Man in a
Suitcase : foreground :
Mark Eden, Richard
Bradford. Callan :
Edward Woodward
(Callan), Russell Hunter
(Lonely). Market in Honey
Lane : Brian Rawlinson
(Danny), John Bennett
(Billy Bush), Peter Birrel
(Jacko Bennett), Pat Nye
(Polly Jessell).
134/135 The Prisoner :
Patrick McGoohan (The
Prisoner), Angelo
Muscat (Butler). The Des
O'Connor Show : Jack
Douglas, Des O'Connor.
136/137 Coronation Street
Wedding : Paul Maxwell
(Sgt. Steve Tanner), Pat
Phoenix (Elsie Tanner).
Never Mind the Quality,
Feel the Width : John
Bluthal (Manny Cohen),
Joe Lynch (Patrick Kelly).

1968
138/139 Please Sir : John
Alderton (Bernard
Hedges), Penny Spencer
(third left, Sharon), Peter
Cleall (Duffy), Liz
Gebhardt (Maureen),
David Barry (Abbott),
Peter Denyer (Dunstable).
140/141 We Have Ways of
Making You Laugh : Dick
Bentley, Frank Muir.
Virgin of the Secret
Service : Veronica Strong
(Mrs. Virginia Cortez),
Clinton Greyn (Robert
Virgin), John Cater (Fred
Doublett). Olympics,
Mexico City. 200m : Peter
Norman (Australia),
Tommie Smith (USA), John
Carlos (USA).
142/143 Nearest and
Dearest : Jimmy Jewel (Eli
Pledge), Hylda Baker
(Nellie Pledge). Tom
Grattan's War : Connie
Merigold (Mrs. Alice
Kirkin), Sally Adcock
(Julie), Michael Howe (Tom
Grattan).
144/145 Playhouse – The
Father : Sybil Thorndike
(Nurse), Patrick Wymark
(Captain). Do Not Adjust
Your Set : Denise Coffey
with Michael Palin, David
Jason, Terry Jones, Eric
Idle, and the Bonzo Dog
Doo-Dah Band. Father,
Dear Father : Ann
Holloway (Karen), Patrick
Cargill (Patrick Glover),
Natasha Pyne (Anna).
146/147 Freewheelers :
Tom Owen (Bill), Mary
Maude (Terry), Gregory
Phillips (Chris). A Man Of
Our Times : Isabel Dean
(Lydia Laing), George
Cole (Max Osborne).

1969
150/151 The Dustbinmen :
Tim Wylton (Eric), Trevor
Bannister (Heavy
Breathing), Bryan Pringle
(Cheese and Egg),
Graham Haberfield
(Winston). Bangelstein's
Boys : Colin Welland, Ray
Smith.
152/153 Stars on Sunday :
Harry Secombe. Doctor in
the House : George Layton
(Paul Collier), Barry Evans
(Michael Upton), Robin
Nedwell (Duncan
Waring). On the Buses :
Stephen Lewis (Insp.), Reg
Varney (Stan Butler), Bob
Grant (Jack).
154/155 Special Branch :
Morris Perry (Charles
Moxon), Derren Nesbit
(Det.-Chief Insp. Jordan),
Alfred Bell (Det.-Sgt. Mills),
Fulton Mackay (Chief Supt.
Inman).
156/157 The Main Chance :
John Stride (David Main),
Anna Palk (Sarah
Courtney). This is Your
Life : The Beverley Sisters,
Eamonn Andrews.

1970
158/159 A Family At War :
Ian Thompson (John
Porter), Lesley Nunnerley
(Margaret Ashton), John
McKelvey (Sefton Briggs),
Trevor Bowen (Tony
Briggs), Coral Atkins
(Sheila Ashton), Colin
Campbell (David Ashton),
Keith Drinkel (Philip
Ashton). Foreground :
Colin Douglas (Edwin
Ashton), Barbara Flynn
(Freda Ashton), Shelagh
Frazer (Jean Ashton).
160/161 Manhunt : Alfred
Lynch (Jimmy), Peter
Barkworth (Vincent), Cyd
Hayman (Nina).
162/163 The Lovers :
Richard Beckinsale
(Geoffrey), Paula Wilcox
(Beryl). Crime of Passion :
John Phillips (Maître
Lacan), Daniel Moynihan
(Maître Savel), Anthony
Newlands (President of
Court). For the Love of
Ada : Wilfred Pickles
(Walter Bingley), Irene
Handl (Ada Cresswell).
166/167 Catweazle :
Geoffrey Bayldon
(Catweazle).

Further details of actors and characters pictured throughout this book.

1971
168/169 **Upstairs, Downstairs :** Pauline Collins (Sarah), Angela Baddeley (Mrs. Bridges), George Innes (Alfred), Gordon Jackson (Mr. Hudson), Evin Crowley (Emily), Brian Osborne (Pearce), Patsy Smart (Roberts), Jean Marsh (Rose). Foreground : David Langton (Richard Bellamy), Rachel Gurney (Lady Marjorie Bellamy).
170/171 **Persuasion :** Richard Vernon (Admiral Croft), Bryan Marshall (Capt. Wentworth).
172/173 **And Mother Makes Three :** David Parfitt (Peter), Wendy Craig (Sally Harrison), Robin Davies (Simon). **The Persuaders :** Roger Moore (Lord Brett Sinclair), Tony Curtis (Danny Wilde).
174/175 **Bless This House :** Sidney James (Sid Abbott), Diana Coupland (Jean Abbott), Sally Geeson (Sally), Robin Stewart (Mike). **The Fenn Street Gang :** Peter Cleall (Eric Duffy), Leon Vitali (Peter Craven), Peter Denyer (Dennis Dunstable), Carol Hawkins (Sharon Eversleigh), Liz Gebhardt (Maureen Bullock), David Barry (Frankie Abbott), Foreground : Jill Kernan (Penny Hedges), John Alderton (Bernard Hedges).

1972
178/179 **Country Matters – The Higgler :** Keith Drinkel.
180/181 **The Strauss Family :** Stuart Wilson (Strauss Jr.). **Van der Valk :** Barry Foster (Van der Valk), Michael Latimer (Kroon). **My Good Woman :** Leslie Crowther (Clive Gibbons), Sylvia Syms (Sylvia Gibbons).
182/183 **Black Beauty :** Judi Bowker (Vicky). **Who Do You Do? :** Peter Goodwright, Freddie Starr. **Sale of the Century** (Celebrity edition) : Arthur Askey, Nicholas Parsons, Sheila Hancock, Jennifer Cresswell, John Alderton. **Shut That Door :** Tessie O'Shea, Larry Grayson. **Love Thy Neighbour :** Kate Williams (Joan Booth), Jack Smethurst (Eddie Booth), Nina Baden-Semper (Barbara Reynolds), Rudolph Walker (Bill Reynolds).
184/185 **Adam Smith :** Andrew Keir (Adam).
186/187 **Emergency – Ward 10 :** John Carlisle and Charles Lamb. **Emmerdale Farm :** Andrew Burt (Jack Sugden), Frazer Hines (Joe Sugden).

1973
190/191 **Long Day's Journey Into Night :** Laurence Olivier (James Tyrone). **Shabby Tiger :** John Nolan (Nick Faunt), Prunella Gee (Anna Fitzgerald). **Beryl's Lot :** Mark Kingston (Tom Humphries), Carmel McSharry (Beryl Humphries).
192/193 **Divorce His : Divorce Hers :** Richard Burton, Elizabeth Taylor (Martin and Jane Reynolds).
194/195 **The Brontes of Haworth :** Michael Kitchen (Branwell Bronte), Ann Penfold (Anne Bronte), Alfred Burke (The Rev. Patrick Bronte), Freda Dowie (Aunt Branwell), Rosemary McHale (Emily), Vickery Turner (Charlotte Bronte).
196/197 **Sam :** John Price (Alan Dakin), Ray Smith (George Barraclough), Barbara Ewing (Dora Wilson), Alethea Charlton (Ethel Barraclough), Kevin Moreton (Sam). **Helen – A Woman of Today :** Diana Hutchinson (Diana Tulley), Christopher Ballantyne (Chris Tulley), Martin Shaw (Frank Tulley), Alison Fiske (Helen Tulley).

1974
200/201 **Intimate Strangers :** Anthony Bate (Harvey Paynter), Patricia Lawrence (Joan Paynter). **Thick As Thieves :** Bob Hoskins (Dobbs), Pat Ashton (Annie), John Thaw (Stan). **The Inheritors :** Peter Egan (Michael Gethin), Robert Urquhart (James, Lord Gethin).
202/203 **Boy Dominic :** Richard Todd (Charles Bulman).
204/205 **The Zoo Gang :** Lilli Palmer (Manouche Roget), John Mills (Tommy Devon), Barry Morse (Alec Marlowe), Brian Keith (Stephen Halliday). **South Riding :** Norman Scace (Rev. Millward Peckover), Barbara Ogilvie (Miss Parsons), Dorothy Tutin (Miss Sarah Burton, MA), Clive Swift (Councillor Alfred Ezekiel Huggins).
206/207 **Rising Damp :** Frances de la Tour (Miss Jones), Don Warrington (Philip Smith), Richard Beckinsale (Hallam), Leonard Rossiter (Rigsby). **Wheeltappers and Shunters Social Club :** Colin Crompton.

1975
210/211 **My Brother's Keeper :** George Layton (Brian Booth), Jonathan Lynn (Pete Booth). **Born Free :** Diana Muldaur and Elsa. **The Stars Look Down :** Ian Hastings (David Fenwick), Susan Tracey (Jenny Sunley).
212/213 **Akenfield :** Ronald Blythe (Vicar), Lyn Brooks (Charlotte Rouse), Garrow Shand (Tom Rouse). **Space 1999 :** Anthony Valentine (alien).
214/215 **Carry On Laughing :** Kenneth Connor, Jack Douglas, Joan Sims. **The Hanged Man :** Colin Blakely (Lew Burnett). **A Place in Europe :** the house and gardens of Vaux-le-Vicomte.

1976
218/219 **Luke's King** Oliver Tobias (Luke Firbeck).
220/221 **Yus My De** Arthur Mullard (Wa Briggs), Queenie W (Lil Briggs).
222/223 **Clayhange** Janet Suzman (Hilda Lessways), Peter M (Edwin Clayhanger
224/225 **Rock Follie** Rula Lenska (Q), Charlotte Cornwell (Anna), Julie Coving (Dee). **The Fosters** Lenny Henry (Sonn Carmen Munro (Vil Isabelle Lucas (Pea Norman Beaton (Sa Lawrie Mark (Benja Sharon Rosita (Shirl **Red Letter Day :** Jac Shepherd (Phil, the Director), Joe Black McGill).
226/227 **The Ghosts Motley Hall :** Nichola Prevost (Fanny), Ar English (Bodkin), Se Flanagan (Matt), Fre Jones (Sir George Uproar), Sheila Stea (The White Lady). **T Feathered Serpent :** Patrick Troughton (Diané Keen (Chimal **Hello Cheeky :** John Junkin, Barry Cryer Brooke-Taylor.
228/229 **Bouquet of Barbed Wire :** Frank Finlay (Peter Manso Susan Penhaligon (P Sorenson). **Death of Informer :** Tom Bell (Kenneth Lennon).

278

The Dame of Sark:
ritton (Colonel Von
ttau), Peter Dyneley
athaway), Celia
n (Sybil Hathaway).
nes and Son: Paula
(Elizabeth Jones),
opher Beeny
ey). Love For Lydia:
artin (Lydia Aspen),
opher Blake (Edward
dson).
 Coronation Street:
Adamson (Len
ugh), Barbara Knox
ittlewood). Robin's
Richard O'Sullivan
 Tripp), Tessa Wyatt
), Tony Britton (James
ls). Philby, Burgess
aclean: Michael Culver
d Maclean), Derek
 (Guy Burgess).
9 Hard Times: Patrick
'Mr. Gradgrind),
y West (Mr.
erby). Devenish: John
Rog Box), Dinsdale
n (Arthur Devenish).
YY Man: Stephen
ey (Spider Scott). Just
m: Adrian Dannatt
am), Bonnie Langford
 Elizabeth Bott).

 Edward and Mrs.
on: Edward Fox
ard VIII), Cynthia Harris
s Simpson), Charles
ng (Ernest Simpson).
3 Lillie: Francesca
(Lillie Langtry), Patrick
Dean le Breton), Anton
rs (Edward Langtry).
rime of Miss Jean
e: Lynsey Baxter (Sandy
er), Geraldine
van (Jean Brodie),
da Kirby (Jenny Gray).
s of Glory: Robin Bevan
am Wordsworth), Susan
rs (Dorothy
sworth).
7 The Old Crowd:
 Dean (Betty), Jill
ett (Stella), Frank
es (Glyn). Spearhead:
older (Sgt. Bilinski),
ge Sweeney (L/Cpl.
), Charles Cork (Pte.
), Gordon Case (Pte.
oe).
1 Enemy At The Door:
 Burke (Oberst Dieter
er), Thelma Whiteley
ly Brown).

1979

252/253 **Danger UXB:**
Anthony Andrews (Lt. Brian
Ash).
254/255 **Flambards:** Alan
Parnaby (William), Sebastian
Abineri (Dick), Steven Grives
(Mark). **Shelley(** Josephine
Tewson (Mrs. Hawkins),
Hywel Bennett (James
Shelley). **Kidnapped:** David
McCallum (Alan Breck
Stewart).
256/257 **The Mallens:** Thomas
Hallam (Squire Thomas
Mallen), John Duttine
(Donald Radlet).
258/259 **Agony:** Maureen
Lipman (Jane Lucas). **Tropic:**
Bobbie Brown (Ena Grant),
Paul Hastings (Johnny
Onions). **The Racing Game:**
Mike Gwilym (Sid Halley).
260/261 **Dick Barton:** Tony
Vogel (Dick Barton), James
Cosmo (Jock Anderson),
Anthony Heaton (Snowey
White). **After Julius:** Faith
Brook (Esme Grace), John
Carson (Felix King). **The
Sound of The Guns:** Richard
Hurndall (General).
262/263 **The Glums:** Jimmy
Edwards (Mr. Glum), Ian
Lavender (Ron), Patricia
Brake (Eth). **The Dancing
Years:** Susan Skipper
(Grete), Anthony Valentine
(Rudi), Celia Gregory
(Maria).

1980

264/265 **Hollywood:**
Recording the roar of the
MGM lion.
266/267 **Why Didn't They Ask
Evans?** Francesca Annis
(Lady Frances Derwent),
James Warwick (Bobby
Jones). **The Further
Adventures of Oliver Twist:**
Daniel Murray (Oliver), John
Fowler (Artful Dodger).
268/269 **Young At Heart:** Sir
John Mills (Albert Collyer),
Meg Jenkins (Ethel Collyer).
The Gentle Touch: Jill
Gascoine (Det. Insp. Maggie
Forbes)
272/273 **The Nesbitts are
Coming:** Arthur White (P.C.
Crowther), Christian Rodska
(Tom), Deirdre Costello
(Marlene), Maggie Jones
(Mrs. Nesbitt), Clive Swift
(Mr. Nesbitt), John Price
(Len).
274/275 **Cribb:** Alan Dobie
(Det. Sgt. Cribb), David
Waller (Det. Insp. Jowett),
William Simons (Det. Con.
Thackeray). **The Spoils of
War:** Back row – Ian Hastings
(Keir), Alan Hunter (Blake),
Nat Jackley (Harry), Leslie
Schofield (Owen). Middle
row – Emily Moore (Peg),
William Lucas (George), Avis
Bunnage (Helen), Madalaine
Newton (Jean). Front row –
Gary Carp (Lovett), John
Francis Foley (Colin).